Ten Keys to
Writing Success

TEN KEYS TO WRITING SUCCESS

by
Donald E. Bower

THE NATIONAL WRITERS PRESS
1987

Printed in the United States of America by
The National Writers Press
1450 South Havana
Aurora, CO 80012

International Standard Book Number: 0-88100-057-4

Library of Congress Catalog Card No. 87-60072

Distributed by
The National Writers Press
1450 So. Havana St.
Aurora, CO 80012

PERMISSIONS

The author acknowledges the cooperation of authors and publishers in giving permission to reproduce portions of their material in *Ten Keys to Writing Success*.

Ausland, Malory, and Callaway, Dorothy. For selections from *Professional Writing*, by Walter S. Campbell. Published by the Macmillan Company.

Dodd, Mead & Company, Inc. For passages from *A Time to Write*, by Loula Grace Erdman.

Doubleday & Company, Inc. For selections from *Techniques of Fiction Writing*, by Leon Surmelian.

Houghton Mifflin Company. For a selection from *The Immigrants*, by Howard Fast. © 1977 by Howard Fast.

Macmillan Publishing Company. For selections from *On Being An Author*, by Vera Brittain; and selections from *The Elements of Style*, by William Strunk, Jr., and E.B. White.

Ober, Harold Associates. For selections from *In Search of Readers*, by Pearl S. Buck. From *The Writer's Book*, compiled by The Author's Guild and published by Harper & Row.

Prentice-Hall, Inc. For selections from *The Magic Key to Successful Writing* by Maxine Lewis.

Souvenir Press, Ltd. For a passage from *The Day The World Ended*, by Gordon Thomas and Max Morgan.

University of Michigan Press, The. For selections from *The Writer and His Craft*, by Roy W. Cowden.

University of Pittsburgh Press. For selections from *A Western Journal: A Daily Log of the Great Parks Trip, June 20-July 2, 1938*, by Thomas Wolfe.

Writer, The. For selections from *The Craft of Novel Writing*, by Julian Green.

Writer's Digest Books. For selections from *The Writer's Survival Guide*, by Jean and Veryl Rosenbaum.

TABLE OF CONTENTS

PREFACE

After spending more than 30 years as an editor, publisher, author and consultant, I decided it was time to share some of my experiences and knowledge and end, once and for all, the myth that there is a magic formula separating the aspiring writer from the successful professional. Houdini, not unlike the computer programmer, would never reveal his illusions to the world. Doctors, lawyers and ham radio operators, talk in a mysterious language comprehensible only to their peers. Ask a fisherman where the rainbow trout are lurking and you'll seldom get a straight answer. Even the fast-food chains keep their formulas for fried chicken and hamburgers a tightly guarded secret.

Writers, on the other hand, are willing to tell the world how they achieved their goal. They don't fear the competition, or worry about creating a literary monster who may ultimately devour them. At a writer's workshop a few years ago, I asked a prominent author why he was so willing to openly discuss how he found his way to the top. "How to do it is an easy thing to explain. But doing it is the difficult part. I'd be surprised if ten percent of the people in this audience have the persistence to become a writer. Out of a thousand who think they want to be writers, less than a dozen are willing to make the sacrifice."

Clive Cussler, addressing a group of about 100 would-be writers, told them, "About half of the people here will start a novel, and of those only half will ever finish it. And of those, another fifty percent will send it out to a publisher once, have it rejected and then let it gather dust in the closet."

In the process of developing this book, I observed that there is no feat of magic involved in becoming a professional writer. As I reviewed my notes and recollections of conversations with dozens of well-known authors it became obvious that anyone with average intelligence and an adequate knowledge of the English language could write publishable material. As one editor told me, "You don't have to be anybody special to make money with a book. All you really need is a catchy idea."

You also need persistence and determination. There is no easy way to the top and if you believe that *Ten Keys to Writing Success*, or any other book on writing offers a panacea, you will be disappointed. Unless you are willing to make a commitment to authorship, unless you have already decided to dedicate your time, effort, energy and imagination and accept the sacrifices and give up the momentary pleasures in your life, all of the volumes available on writing technique will bring you naught but failure.

With more than two thousand books in print on the subject of writing, it took a lot of soul-searching as well as some imagination before I decided to add to this abundance. I concluded, finally, that there was a similarity in most of the existing books on writing and a serious lack in one particular area. Typical titles are *How to Write a Novel; How to Write Short Stories; How to Write Articles; Writing and Selling a Nonfiction Book; How to Write Mysteries; How to Write Contemporary Romances; How to Write and Sell Poetry; Writing for Television;* and many more. The concentration was primarily on the mechanics and technique. So many books exist, in fact, that an entire volume of more than 400 pages lists 298 titles relating to writing the novel; more than 200 titles on writing poetry; and nearly 400 books and articles on writing television and movie scripts. This book, *The Writer's Advisor*, compiled by Leland G. Alkire, includes 4,259 reference works on various subjects of writing and it is by no means complete.

For almost half a century I've been involved in writing, as a publisher, magazine and book editor, a freelance writer, workshop planner and speaker, and director of one of the largest and oldest national writers' organizations in the U.S.

I've read well over a thousand books and articles related to creative writing, but the one book that helped me most in my career had little to do with writing—Norman Vincent Peale's, *The Power of Positive Thinking*.

Writing can be a discouraging and disappointing experience, and endless failures and rejections almost always precede even a minor degree of success. Before one becomes involved in studying techniques, attending classes, and participating in workshops, he or she should assume a positive mental attitude. Few books about writing consider the psychological and philosophical aspects, essential ingredients in the literary aspirant's psyche.

The keys to unlock the door to the sought-after achievement are found in the heart and the spirit, the determination, the subconscious (or unconscious) mind, the imagination and inspiration, plus the persistence of the writer. You must believe in yourself. You must have self-confidence as well as a fervent desire to make it in this business.

Some of the questions *Ten Keys to Writing Success* will answer are: What happens to you in the course of becoming a writer? What impact does writing have on you, on your personality, and on your lifestyle? What purpose does your writing serve? Why have you chosen to be a writer? How should you select your goals? How are you going to deal with your success? Are you psychologically adapted to be a writer?

Although the main thrust of this book relates to the aspiring writer, the experienced professional will discover some secrets he never knew, or has forgotten, that may add to his achievements. I hope I've succeeded in providing the encouragement you need, and that in the dark days when the dreaded writer's block invades your psyche, you will review some of the chapters (especially Key One) in this volume.

You'll find in the following pages, in addition to writing techniques, how to live with yourself (and your family) as a writer, how to improve your writing style, how to deal with outside pressures, depression, and success. And you'll also learn how to write and sell a story.

Each of the ten keys I've included has been developed through the approach used in my writing career, and I'm convinced that these ten keys can provide you with a path to the pinnacle you seek, and may make some of your dreams come true.

—*Donald E. Bower*
Aurora, Colorado

Key One

The Positive Frame of Mind

"Dear Author: Your manuscript has been accepted and our contract is enclosed. Our check for $10,000 against advance royalties will be forwarded as soon as we receive your signed copy of the agreement."

So much for the future. So much for Utopia. You have challenges to face and obstacles to overcome before this dream comes true. Prior to starting the task at hand, you need to answer some questions truthfully and objectively. If you don't have the right answers, you can save time by putting this book back on the shelf.

Score

1. Are you serious about a writing career? If your answer is yes, score 10 points. _____

2. Do you enjoy writing? If your answer is yes, score 10 points. _____

3. Why do you want to write?
   a) I have something important to say. Score 15 points. _____
   b) I want to communicate my ideas to others. Score 10 points. _____
   c) I want to entertain my readers. Score 10 points. _____
   d) I feel that I'm a good story teller. Score 10 points. _____
   e) I want to write for money. Score 5 points. _____
   f) I think it's an easy way to make a living. Score 0 points. _____

g) I want to become a celebrity. Score 0
   points.   _____
h) I want to write to please myself. Score 0
   points.   _____
i) I'm willing to devote my time and energy
   to become successful, and willing to sacrifice the momentary pleasures that may
   distract me from my ultimate goal. Score
   30 points.   _____

A perfect score is 100. If you scored 60 or more, you may have what it takes to be a writer. For those who are already practicing writers, consider this test as a measure of your ability versus your accomplishments.

Ten Keys to Writing Success will provide you with the psychological attitudes, procedures, knowledge, and tools you need to reach your objective.

For those who scored less than 60, it's been nice knowing you. Enjoy yourself, go fishing, play some golf, and loan this book to a friend.

One of the questions, "Why do you want to write?" listed the most common reasons, but not the only reasons. How many writers and would-be writers can relate to Louisa Mae Alcott who wrote to avoid a rather unpleasant occupation? Or Dorothy Parker who claimed that she wrote to win the attention of the opposite sex, and James Branch Cabell who wrote for his own diversion. Balzac wrote to be famous. Samuel Johnson, O. Henry, Murray Hazlett Brennan, and a host of others wrote for the most obvious reason of all: to make money. Thomas Wolfe wrote because it was a compulsion. As Somerset Maugham noted in *The Summing Up:* "We do not write because we want to; we write because we must."

We can find a common denominator which underlies all of the other reasons. We write through a desire to communicate. As historian Rex Alan Smith told his audience at a writer's conference, "Writers are the communicators of the world. It is through writing that we know who we are." The history of man and nature is recorded in our writings, from the days of our earliest ancestors who scratched out hieroglyphics on the walls, to the monks who spent lifetimes laboriously writing by hand volumes that described the world as it was centuries ago, and finally, in 1438, to Johannes Gutenberg's invention of the printing press and the advent of moveable type that led to the mass production of books.

Some twenty or so years ago Norman Cousins lectured a group of students on the subject, "In Defense of a Writing Career," in which he emphasized the role of new writers. He said, "There is need for writers who can restore to writing its powerful tradition of leadership in crisis . . . There is no more essential and nobler task for writers—established writers, new writers, aspiring writers—than to regard themselves as spokesmen for human destiny."

To pursue your plan to become an author, you must make this commitment: that you will write honestly and objectively in your efforts to communicate those ideas and ideals about which you feel strongly and which will be a contribution to our society. The contribution may be to educate, to amuse, to improve the reader's lifestyle, or to offer a pleasant diversion.

Unless you are convinced that writing is a vital part of your life and that you shall remain unsatisfied until you have fulfilled this creative urge, you will probably give up in despair, replacing the typewriter or word processor with a new sports car, a sailboat, a large-screen TV, or a trip to the Bahamas.

Having accepted the challenge, you must prepare yourself for the difficulties, for the disappointments, and for the mental and psychological roadblocks that you will encounter. You must think affirmatively. In no other career is the power of positive thinking more essential. You must repeat, day in and day out, "I can write. I can be a successful writer. I will be a successful writer." Build up your ego and convince yourself that you are a writer. Visualize your future success and what it will mean to you—the fame, the fortune, the pleasures and the excitement that your long-sought achievements will bring.

Avoid the fear of failure by putting it out of your mind. As Emily Dickinson wrote, "You never know how tall you are, till you are called to rise." At a writer's workshop I listened to Beverly Anderson Nemiro, a motivational speaker and co-author of *Single After Fifty: How to Have the Time of Your Life*, suggest that a writer should have a bulletin board above the typewriter filled with press clippings about famous authors, replacing the author's photograph with his or her own.

Keep a record or a scrapbook of all of the good things that have happened to you—awards you may have won, stories or articles that you have published, great moments or victories in competitions—and keep it by your side, referring to it during those periods of depression, when the creative flow seems to have evaporated.

These may seem to be artificial devices, gimmicks perhaps more appropriate in a huckster's manual than in a serious book about creative art, but they work. You must have indelibly etched in your mind that you will succeed, that nothing will destroy your self-confidence, your convictions. Picture yourself as a success. Norman Vincent Peale wrote, "Make a true estimate of your own ability, then raise it ten percent." You might consider raising it twenty percent, theorizing that your talents will be increased substantially once you have taken the first step toward becoming a writer. Just as a law student increases his stature the day he receives his degree, even though he still has to pass the bar, so a neophyte writer increases his capabilities the day he decides to become an author.

The famous psychologist, William James, stressed that "Our belief at the beginning of a doubtful undertaking [writing is certainly a doubtful undertaking] is the one thing that insures the successful outcome of your venture."

When moments of depression overtake you, and they will, think of all of the good things that you have going for you. Contemplate the wonderful times you have had on vacations, your family relationships, your health, those pleasurable hours with your children, the challenges you've met and overcome. Build up your ego. Have faith in yourself.

Visualize yourself as a success. Close your eyes and allow the image of a great writer to flash upon the screen, someone you recognize as the person whose image is reflected in your mirror each morning. See yourself as the center of attention in the writer's world, saying to that vast audience of your readers, "I am the center of the universe and all things revolve around me."

Norman Vincent Peale believes that "a major key to success in this life, to attaining that which you deeply desire, is to be completely released and throw all there is of yourself into . . . any project in which you are engaged." You must have both faith in yourself and the determination to succeed. On a small card that will fit in your wallet, write these words: "I don't believe in defeat. I will succeed." And refer to it every day at your appointed time to write.

Before you finalize your decision to become a writer, recognizing both the agony and the ecstacy, ask yourself if you are mentally cut out for this profession. To make it in the writing business, you need affirmative answers to these questions:

1. Do I enjoy reading?
2. Do I have a love affair with words?
3. Can I create original ideas, or fresh approaches to subjects that may not be new, but are significant or timely?
4. Do I have an inquiring mind?
5. Am I a good observer?
6. Am I a good listener?
7. Do I have a strong desire to communicate my ideas to others?
8. Am I willing to sacrifice social pleasures and substitute the lonely moments endured by a writer?
9. Do I have a sense of literary values?
10. Do I have the perseverance to continue in the face of rejection?
11. Am I ready to start?

Having made the decision to pursue the *Ten Keys to Writing Success*, you will find in the following sections a step-by-step procedure that will guide you through this complicated maze and help you achieve the goals you have set.

You must create the proper environment, your own little writer's world. If you have a study (a spare bedroom will do), arrange it so that most of the equipment and materials you need will be at your fingertips. There should be an ample-sized desk, a typewriter or word processor (in which case you'll need a printer as well), plenty of paper, a large wastebasket, bookcases with a special section reserved for the books that apply to the particular project you are working on, a file cabinet and adequate lighting.

At the same time, avoid having any distracting elements in the room—television set, extra chairs for visitors, chest of drawers, or a closet filled with the family wardrobe. Your studio should be as far removed from the rest of the house as possible, and it should be your private room. Your spouse and children must be made to understand that you are not to be interrupted when you are in your private sanctuary. If necessary, put a "Do Not Disturb" sign on the door.

Another preliminary step is to establish a set of rules and follow them faithfully. Plan a schedule for writing, which does not necessarily have to be the same hour each day. Resolve that you will be at your writing desk and that you will remain there for a certain length of time. It may be only thirty minutes, at least in the beginning, but you must adhere to the schedule. Obtain a desk calendar and note the dates and times you plan to be at your typewriter. Consider these commitments as important as an appointment you have with your doctor, your attorney or your tax consultant. If you fail to follow the rules you have set, you may lack the discipline required of a writer.

Before you start on a specific project, review your past, the jobs you have held, the people you know, the hobbies you enjoy, the problems you have had and those you have overcome. As an exercise, write a summary of your life, a brief autobiography. Include details of special occasions such as birthdays, anniversaries, reunions, descriptions of places in which you have lived or visited, memorable times with your family, neighbors and friends.

Another exercise that you will find useful, not only as a writing experience, but also as an important part of your research in later writing projects, is the keeping of a journal. This can be in the form of a daily record of your activities, world events or local happenings. If you have made a new acquaintance, describe his or her appearance, his or her attire, your impressions, your concept of what this person is like. Imagine how he would react in different situations, and conjecture about the kind of life he leads, problems he may have had. Carry a notebook with you and jot down ideas as you go about your daily routine. If you visit a restaurant, write a description of the room, the atmosphere, the food that is served. These details may one day add the touch of reality to a book you are writing or an article you're preparing.

Note how Howard Fast adds reality and atmosphere with his description of food in *The Immigrants:* "Seated next to her at one of the tables on the lawn, the air full of the smell of roasting pork, a great platter . . . in front of them, so tender that it was crumbling, flanked with sweet potatoes and little bundles of meat in green ti leaves . . ."

When writing my first travel book, *Roaming the American West*, I not only visited the areas about which I was writing, but made extensive notes at the sites themselves, noting all of the physical aspects and tape recording conversations with the natives of the region as well as the tour guides. I also accumulated as much material as I could find relating to the history of the area, including as part of my research rare booklets from local libraries or gift shops. But I found, when I started writing, that it was the personal notes and anecdotes that made my book come to life.

Perhaps the best prototype of a writer's notebook is Thomas Wolfe's *A Western Journal*, a daily log of his trip through the great parks of the western United States in 1938, shortly before his death. As the jacket copy states, "It is peculiarly Wolfe—his emotions, his wonder, his discovery, his large appetite for everything he could see or imagine." Wolfe writes of ". . . The little slaughtered wild things in the road—in Oregon, in California, across the desert, going up—through Utah, in Idaho, Wyoming, and Montana—the little crushed carcasses of the gophers, chipmunks, jackrabbits, birds—in the hot bright western light the black crows picking at some furry mangled little carcass on the hot road—rises and flaps slowly, *vauntingly* away as the car approaches."

Your journal doesn't have to be Wolfeian, but it should include your impressions and feelings, as well as the mundane activities of the day. Recall much more than the ordinary routine. You may wish to write about unusual weather phenomena. If it was overcast and windy, describe the atmosphere, the bending of the trees, the billowing shapes of the clouds. Describe the rain.

Was it a misty day that had a depressing influence on you, or a summer cloudburst that caused the gutters to overflow, followed by a burst of sunshine and the appearance of a rainbow in the West? If it was a winter snowfall, describe how the snowflakes piled up in drifts or changed the pine trees into giant ice cream cones. Each day brings new experiences, but these are soon forgotten unless you have recorded them. Faithfully noting these events in your journal should be another essential part of your daily routine as a writer.

Not only may your notes provide important background information for future writing projects, but starting each session making these entries may supply the necessary stimulation for getting the creative juices flowing when you turn to the manuscript on which you are currently working, thus avoiding the panic referred to as 'writer's block'.

And getting started is one of the difficulties a writer faces. Stephen Leacock, in *How to Write*, suggests that you not start anywhere in particular. "Begin at the end: begin in the middle, but *begin.*" Don't be hesitant if the right words don't seem to come. Remember that you are writing a draft, that your words are not etched in stone, and until you reach a final revision you are writing for your own eyes only. If possible, let your thoughts come from your subconscious, or as Dorothea Brande calls it, your unconscious. Let the words flow as effortlessly as possible. Should you be unable to think of the right word, the exact word, leave a blank and then continue. Should you find a section of the story that impedes your progress, skip it, and come back to it at a later time. Consider yourself a scientist in a laboratory, experimenting with a hundred different formulas. Should the first one fail, you can try another in the next draft.

If, at your appointed time to write, you find yourself in a mental block, relax, draw on your subconscious, write anything that comes into your head—a dream you've had, perhaps, or just gibberish that has no particular meaning, more nonsense than sense. You may find some useful gem in your free-flowing thoughts, or a stimulation that will remove the writer's block.

You must write at your scheduled times. Finding excuses is a fatal flaw. Maxine Lewis points out, "The first thing that makes you not want to write is the frustration that is bound to result when the doors of expression do not fly open at the touch of a hand." Too often the beginning writer finds reasons for not writing. Housework to be done, shopping, mowing the lawn, or cleaning out the garage are unacceptable alibis in the writer's potpourri of excuses.

No writer ever lived who did not suffer from this malady. When one reads the biographies or autobiographies of such famous literary figures as Charles Dickens, Somerset Maugham and Ernest Hemingway, it becomes apparent that even the greatest and most prolific authors have been victims of the writer's block. The aspiring writer should recognize that his problems are not unique. "A beginning writer needs advice, companionship, and the sharing of the experience of writing. . . . When he realizes that his difficulties and frustrations are the lot of all writers, he may be considerably happier," writes Vera Brittain in *On Being An Author*.

One suggestion that may eliminate the problems of getting started, Vera Brittain believes, is "to always arrange . . . to finish your day's work at some point where it is easy to begin again tomorrow. If the next stage of your book is a difficult paragraph, or the opening of a recalcitrant chapter, your natural reluctance to start will waste much time. . . . If you know exactly what you are going to say next, you will sit down to your task with enthusiasm."

One of the more proficient romance writers, Maggie Osborne, tells her writing classes that the thought of writing a 70,000-word book always appalled her, and she overcomes the obstacle by considering one chapter at a time. Some writers prefer to think of their project on a single page basis. When you realize that by writing only one page a day (250 to 300 words) you can complete a 90,000 word book every year, the task becomes less formidable.

No single formula or device applies to all writers, and it may take a lot of experimenting to determine what works for you. Friedrich Schiller kept over-ripe apples in his desk, needing the smell of rotting fruit to stir up his creative juices. Thomas Wolfe preferred to scribble his voluminous flow of words on the top of a refrigerator, and Mark Twain liked to write lying in bed.

A friend of mine writes while sitting in a bathtub filled with luke-warm water. I prefer soft music in the background to detract from the solitude.

Use whatever it takes to get started. Once under way, the momentum will build and, like a locomotive achieving full speed, the words will flow and the excitement will race through your veins as your creativity is transformed into sentences, paragraphs and chapters, until you reach your own denouement.

Norman Cousins noted that writing "is amazingly difficult work at times . . . but . . . it is the sweetest agony known to man. This is the one fatigue that produces inspiration, an exhaustion that exhilarates." No writer worth his salt was ever able to escape the torment of creation, but for those who who do not allow the difficulties to destroy their faith and their determination to reach their goal, the rewards are sure to come.

Having developed a positive attitude and confidence in your abilities as well as your will to succeed, it is now time to define your interests and establish your goals.

Key Two

Defining Your Interests

You've made the decision to become a writer, or a better writer. To determine more specifically the kind of writer you should be it's necessary to evaluate your abilities and this requires some self-analysis, an objective look inside your pysche. Write your responses to the following questions and refer to your answers when you reach Key Six: A Time for Decision.

Self-Analysis Test

1. How would you describe your background? What was your environment like as a child?

2. What were some of the more unusual experiences in your life?

3. What activities do you most enjoy? Are you an outdoorsman, a backpacker who seeks out mountain trails, a cross country skier who likes to get off the beaten track, a photography enthusiast, a stamp collector, an antique fanatic, a history buff or an armchair participant in sports? A writer friend of mine whose hobby happens to be model railroading has sold over a dozen articles related to this avocation. Another acquaintance designs and builds unusual lamps in his spare time. "I've sold stories to six different publications about this hobby of mine. Even though it wasn't intended to be income producing, I've ended up this past year with a substantial profit from the magazines, plus selling over a thousand dollars' worth of lamps."

4. Do you enjoy traveling? When you travel, are you an observer rather than a participant? Are you more interested in people than places?

5. What kind of friends do you have? Are most of your acquaintances job related? Are they neighbors? What do you have in common? Where and how did you meet them?

6. What about your social life? At a party, are you an introvert or an extrovert? Do you participate in discussions or other proceedings? Do you make a serious effort to learn what makes other people tick?

7. What courses in school were your favorites? Which did you like the least?

8. What kind of magazines and books do you like to read?

9. What kind of jobs have you had? Which ones were the most satisfying? Why? Which were the least satisfying? Why?

Again and again you will hear writers say, "Write about things you know." James Michener was an historian first and a novelist second. Louis L'Amour's western books have the ring of authenticity because ranching was a part of his life long before he began writing about the West.

The broader your range of experience the greater your scope as a writer will be. Your responses to this quiz may offer clues as to the direction your writing may take, but will not provide you with a definitive answer concerning the format or subject matter of your literary endeavors. It won't, for example, tell you that you are a natural born novelist, playwright or poet. You must make these decisions after you have completed your apprenticeship, convinced, of course, that being an author is one of your primary ambitions.

One of the advantages of attempting a career as an author is that writing can be done at home, and even taught at home. It can be learned while working at another profession. You don't need a license, nor do you need to pass any examinations or join a union. While a college education may be helpful, it is not essential. Charles Dickens, Jane Austen, the Brontes, Robert Burns, Walt Whitman, Virginia Woolf and Anthony Trollope were a few of many who never received a degree.

It's possible, also, to write in any environment. Jane Austen created her masterpieces while surrounded by her family and with very little privacy. Newspaper columnists write amid the constant clatter of typewriters, printers and teletype machines. Malcolm Braly wrote while spending 17 years in San Quentin prison. He had no typewriter and did not know how to type. According to an interview by Roger H. Smith in *Publishers Weekly*, Braly "got a clerical job in the prison, typing file cards, first by the hunt-and-peck system. . . . His own writing he did longhand in his cell at night and transcribed his notes in between his official writing chores." If you really have the desire, the urge, you can achieve your objectives as a writer, regardless of the handicaps that may surround you. Just don't expect too much too soon.

In establishing goals, beginning writers often set their sights too high and find themselves unable to cope with the disappointments that follow. When considering your opportunities, look for the easiest markets, the least competitive. These will also probably be the lowest paying as well, but it is more essential to obtain published credits, to see your name in print, than to strive for big paychecks.

At the age of fourteen, I wrote accounts of sandlot baseball games and submitted them to the local paper. I still recall my excitement when I saw my first effort in print. Of course there was no payment, but the intangible rewards were worth far more than money. During my university days I wrote for the college daily and worked on the *Lincoln Journal* (Nebraska) at night, rewriting wire service releases. Later I wrote articles for specialized trade journals, magazines like *American Motel Management* and *Super Service Station*. At that time in my life, I was traveling extensively and became aware of the shortcomings of motel and service station operations. Based on my experiences, I wrote articles relating to the improvement of these facilities. We take for granted the amenities available in motels today, but in the fifties it was rare to find a facility with a restaurant or a swimming pool. Two of my suggestions that caught on were the installation of a small coffee percolator in each guest room, and serving a continental breakfast free of charge in the motel lobby.

During my days as a newspaper editor, I covered the crime beat in addition to my editorial duties, and soon discovered that with a little rewriting some of the more bizarre news events (usually rape or murder) could be adapted, with a bit of fictionalizing, for magazines like *Official Detective, True Police*

Cases and *Amazing Detective*. By adding a few complications, I expanded these into paperback mysteries, for which I was paid the lump sum of $500. From the beginning, I exploited my own experiences and knowledge (and law enforcement contacts) as a basis for this phase of my writing career.

Your goals, and how you go about achieving them, is a decision only you can make. But by examining the autobiographical notes you have completed as an earlier exercise, you should have some idea as to the direction you should take, and where to begin.

As a starting point, you might consider writing letters to the editor of your local paper about issues you believe are significant and controversial. Another possibility: A part-time writer or correspondent for a small newspaper. The pay might be low, but you will gain the experience of writing for publication, meeting deadlines and writing on a regular basis. Many successful writers started out selling to technical journals or business publications, a field largely overlooked but one that has proven to be a steady and lucrative source of income. With more and more specialized businesses, the trade journal market is flourishing. It may not be the glamorous kind of writing that you visualized, but it is a field filled with opportunities. If you are with a company that subscribes to trade publications, you may have a ready-made market. Are there procedures or practices in your operation that could be applied to the industry as a whole? Examine a few issues of these publications and you'll probably uncover an idea that has been overlooked and about which you can write with a minimum amount of research.

Seldom does a beginning writer have the resources to devote full time to his creative efforts, and the choice of a 'bread-and-butter' position should be carefully selected. Vera Brittain, in the book, *On Being An Author*, advises, "the work that accompanies your start as a writer should be . . . as 'neutral' as possible. It should involve an occupation in which you are unlikely to become emotionally entangled, and will therefore find easy to relinquish." She suggests that you choose a job that may give you experience you can use in your writing. In her case, for example, she became a nurse during the first World War . . . "Because of it I have been able to describe illness, injury and death with an expert knowledge that I could not have otherwise acquired."

Successful authors who held part-time jobs and started at the bottom includes many of the most famous: Nathaniel Hawthorne was a frustrated writer, earning a pittance writing for the *Salem Gazette*, the *New England Magazine*, *The Token*, and other small, little-known magazines. He suffered one disappointment after another and only his confidence and persistence eventually brought him recognition. Sherwood Anderson supported himself for years by writing advertising copy in a Chicago agency. Thomas Hardy, Joseph Conrad, D.H. Lawrence and H.G. Wells kept themselves alive during the early years by writing potboilers and short stories for the pulps. Clive Cussler wrote the major portion of his first best-seller, *Raise the Titanic*, while drawing unemployment checks following his dismissal from an advertising agency.

Many writers start as teachers, newspaper reporters or editors, jobs related to writing or communications in one form or another. But some were involved in unrelated occupations: Anthony Trollope worked in the post office, St. John Ervine was an insurance salesman, Somerset Maugham and A.J. Cronin planned careers in the medical profession, and Thomas Hardy studied to be an architect.

Starting your writing career on a part-time basis, with other sources of income, allows you the enjoyment of creation without feeling the pressures of providing a salary to support yourself and your family. Being financially independent, however, doesn't mean you should write just for the fun of it.

A frequent mistake made by many beginners, and one that leads to frustration and disappointment, is to write for the sake of writing, without any thought for the marketplace. Most professionals agree that "you must write for a specific market if you are to sell what you write." Typical is this comment made by one of the speakers at a writer's workshop: "The problem of writing to please yourself is that you are too easily pleased."

I overheard a discussion between two writers, both successful in their own genres. One, a writer of novels of espionage and international intrigue, insisted that the only reason for writing at all was to please the reader. The other, a writer of historical novels and a Pulitzer-prize winner, was equally insistent that you should write for the satisfaction of self-expression. Although it would appear they were diametrically opposed, I agree with Pearl S. Buck when she commented that most novels may be written as a means of self expression, but, she adds, "It is doubtful whether even the necessity for self-expression is wholly satisfied if readers are lacking. . . . Communication, for a writer, means readers."

For the novice, such philosophic observations are academic. Whether you feel you are writing for yourself or for some unseen public, you should concentrate on writing honestly, to the very best of your ability. If you don't believe in the words you are putting on paper, you are being untrue to yourself. Even if your creative efforts are published, you will never feel the satisfaction that is achieved through a dedication to writing honestly. Take pride in your writing. Believe Shakespeare: "To thine ownself be true." Having made such a commitment, the odds are in your favor that you will obtain a degree of success, regardless of the creative area you may have selected.

Study the magazines you plan to write for. Key Number Nine, "Selling What You Write," will provide the necessary methodology for marketing your manuscripts. For now, you should learn how to analyze a magazine or periodical. Read the table of contents, as well as the stories and articles, and study the advertisements. Don't overlook the importance of the advertising. Who is the advertiser trying to reach? After all, it's possible that millions of dollars were spent in market research to determine the typical reader of that publication. All of this information is available to you free.

Peruse the letters to the editor, and the editorials. Visualize the typical reader of that magazine and write your own profile of this reader. If you subscribe to the magazines you plan to write for, your study problem is simpler. If you are not a subscriber, you can refer to them in your public library or purchase copies at a second hand bookstore. However, editors and editorial policies frequently change, so confine your analyses to recent issues of the publications you are considering.

Pay special attention to the blurbs that usually appear on the front cover of a magazine to give you a clue as to which stories or articles the editors apparently feel have the most appeal to readers. Don't merely read the stories, but study them sentence by sentence. What about the lead, the opening paragraphs? Does there appear to be a pattern in the stories or articles, a certain style, a particular format? Some editors want an article to start with an anecdote, while others prefer that the purpose of the piece be made evident in the very first paragraph. Another exercise that will prove helpful is to select one of the articles (or stories) and, based on the title alone, write your opening, then compare it with the story as it appeared in the magazine.

Various market directories are published on a regular basis and in most of these you will find some editorial direction. We'll discuss specific directories later. Remember that the magazine editors' comments are guidelines at best; if you plan to write for these publications, you should obtain and study actual copies. Trade journals or in-house magazines may not be available on the newsstand, in which case you can obtain sample copies by writing to the publisher.

Magazines relating to book publishing are also available. *Publisher's Weekly*, the bible of the publishing industry, lists forthcoming books in each issue, with a brief review of each book. Study these titles to determine what different houses are publishing. Again, close examination of the advertisements will be of tremendous help, since they indicate the kind of books that various publishers are promoting. If you wish to write for a particular publisher, send for a copy of its latest book catalog. Visit your favorite bookstore, see what books are being featured and note who is publishing them. While browsing, take some extra time to read the flap copy. Since this is usually written by the marketing experts, it provides you with valuable information as to the segment of the reading public that publisher is trying to reach.

Regardless of the markets you have chosen, you should always have in the back of your mind what impact you want your writing to have on the reader. Is your primary purpose to instruct him, convince him, advise him, inspire him? Or is it, perhaps, merely to amuse him?

Pearl Buck, in a piece called "In Search of Readers," written for *The Writer's Book* in 1950, divided writers into two categories. "One is the kind who wants the select reader, the gourmet in style. This writer cries down the mass magazine and the reprint house. . . . The second kind of writer . . . has a sneaking and unalterable fondness for the crowd . . . When I sit down to write a book I find myself writing about the behavior not of a Proust but of a garage keeper or a grocer, a peasant or a bandit."

What kind of a writer are you going to be? You will find that your talents are not manufactured, but are as instinctive as those of a bird that travels south in the winter, or a salmon that swims upstream to spawn. If you should wander through a library, you will find yourself concentrating in a certain section of the stacks. What you read, the activities you enjoy, the friends you enjoy, all determine the kind of writing you will naturally do.

Before deciding upon a particular writing project, indulge in some solitary contemplation. As John Galsworthy said, the most fruitful thing for a writer to do is engage in quiet brooding. Avoid the temptation to rush to the typewriter, disciplining yourself instead to store up the knowledge you've acquired and the memories you may not have recorded in your notebook but which are recorded in your mind, in your subconscious. Allow yourself to get worked up about your subject until you reach a point where it seethes within you like a boiling cauldron.

When the desire to write becomes overwhelming and you have your story clearly in mind, the time has arrived to transform it into words. This is the springboard that will enable your creative ideas to flow naturally, easily, and in all probability, more convincingly. If you can write spontaneously, with enthusiasm, you can create the illusion of reality that will in turn capture the attention of your readers. Whether writing fiction or nonfiction, you must convince the reader of the authenticity of the situation. Your reader must feel the tension that you have created. The problem your characters face must be both serious and believable. Once the writer's credibility is in doubt, the chance to create an illusion will disappear, and the reader's interest will vanish.

Once you have mastered these techniques (which are vital to your success) you must avoid the temptation to become overconfident. A writer should not delude himself concerning his career. Fame and fortune are reserved for the very few, and even for them it may be long in coming. As Vera Brittain notes, you will, after writing for a few years with a few successes, "look back and remember the richness of your long experience. . . . You recall those radiant moments . . . which came with the sudden changing of your consciousness, and the breathless capture of the right word in which to convey your illumination to others."

You will discover, as you enjoy your initial successes, that your goals will change, or should if the seed you planted is to flourish. Constantly analyze your progress and seek higher mountains to climb. Should you find yourself in a state of contentment, resting in the lap of euphoria, you will have reached your pinnacle, and as the saying goes, "You're on your way down from there."

The real champions in this world are those who are constantly striving toward higher goals, who are not satisfied until they have reached the top of the mountain. Famous tennis players, like Jimmy Connors, John McEnroe and Bjorn Borg, have every reason to be content with their achievements; but even when they've achieved the number one rating in the world, they continue those long hours of practice, constantly striving to improve. A victory at Wimbledon is merely another challenge. For the champion golfer, winning the Masters is just one more step toward a victory at the British Open. For the Olympic competitor, winning a gold medal adds to the determination to achieve two or three or four. To be a real champion, one must constantly seek a higher goal.

Judith Applebaum and Nancy Evans state in their best-selling book, *How to Get Happily Published*, ". . . If you set your goals wisely, with full comprehension of the framework that surrounds their realization, we believe that you'll find an unprecedented degree of fulfillment in getting published, and that you'll encounter serendipitous pleasures. . . . Using your own wits and your own energies provides an especially satisfying way to ensure that the profoundly personal act which writing constitutes comes finally to fruition."

The successful writer cannot, must not, remain on a plateau.

If you must rest on your laurels, let it be a brief respite before establishing new and higher objectives. It is the challenge one accepts that separates the champion from the also-ran. How to deal with success is the subject of Key Ten, the final and perhaps most difficult happening a writer has to face. But we have a long way to go before this illusive problem confronts us.

Key Three

Preparing to Be a Writer

One of the advantages of pursuing a career in writing is that it requires no formal education or special license. Many beginners interpret this to mean there is no need for preparation. Doctors, lawyers, accountants, computer programmers, secretaries, bricklayers, plumbers, mechanics, and musicians spend years in training and then must serve an apprenticeship to become accepted as practitioners of their craft. Writers, likewise, must be willing to study, to learn, to serve their apprenticeship before they can expect recognition. Those who decide to become writers because "it's an easy way to make a living" are deluding themselves.

Key Number One stressed the importance of preparing yourself mentally and building confidence and self-assurance. This is the first step in your training program, and a phase that is very personal and subjective. You must depend upon others as you continue your preparation to be a writer. But do not expect miracles when you seek outside help. The majority of creative writing instructors, and most of the books you read about writing, will start by saying that they cannot teach you how to write. *Ten Keys to Writing Success* is no exception. In many ways you must be your own tutor, although writing classes and books on writing can provide you with some of the procedures, techniques and guidelines, and introduce you to a vast body of knowledge that will make your learning experience easier.

Writers, especially in the early stages, are besieged with offers that seem to offer instant fame and fortune. Whether it be correspondence courses, 'literary agents', 'publishers', 'song producers', or poetry contests, many are scams designed to part the freelance writer from his hard-earned dollars. Unfortunately the writer often loses more than money, ending up wasting time and being frustrated and disappointed, as well as disillusioned.

There is no positive way to determine whether a service being offered is reliable, but generally literary agents who advertise in the writers' magazines are suspect. Likewise, book publishers who solicit your manuscript are, for the most part, considered as 'vanity presses', more than willing to print your book for a substantial fee. Royalty publishers are overwhelmed with unsolicited manuscripts and would not, with rare exceptions, advertise for authors. Poetry competitions which require that you purchase an anthology as a prerequisite to having your contribution published, should also be avoided.

Home study writing courses can be extremely helpful, but again you must choose with care. Before deciding to enroll, obtain as much information as you can from students who have taken a particular writing course, the background of the instructors and the length of time the sponsors have been in business.

Normally, courses offered by colleges and universities are legitimate and worthwhile. The Writer's Digest School provides excellent instruction in various phases of writing. The National Writers School curriculum includes correspondence courses in fiction and nonfiction and, like the Writer's Digest School, has been operating for a long time. The *Literary Market Place* (referred to as LMP) publishes an extensive listing of colleges offering writing courses, as well as some that can be taken by correspondence. A few of the better known courses are offered by Columbia University, City University of New York Graduate Center, University of Southern California, University of Illinois, and Washington University in St. Louis.

In most larger cities, writing courses are available through schools and colleges as part of their extension services or adult education programs. The advantage of attending classes is the one-on-one relationship with the instructor and the rapport you may develop with your peers.

Attending writers' workshops has many pluses, both for the professional and the aspiring writer. Again, you must be selective and wary. A well-run workshop or seminar with qualified leaders can be a turning point in your writing career. But learn as much as you can about the conference before signing up. Are the subjects covered those in which you are most interested? What about the background of the speakers? Will there be round-table sessions to give you the opportunity for discussions with workshop leaders in an informal atmosphere? Are there editors or others on the program who may be instrumental as contacts when you are submitting manuscripts to magazines or book publishers?

Both *The Writer* and *Writer's Digest* list most of the writers' workshops in their spring issues. With over 200 of these get-togethers each year, you should be able to find a suitable conference in your area, although in some cases it may pay dividends to travel a few more miles to make contacts with editors who may prove especially helpful.

The typical agenda for a workshop might read like this:

Writing the Novel
Writing the Nonfiction Book
Writing and Selling Poetry
Writing for Television
The Role of the Literary Agent
Turning Rejections Into Paychecks
The Techniques of Writing
Successful Article Writing
Writing for Children
Writing for Women
Writing for the Markets

Only some of the subjects covered will concern you, but it doesn't hurt to attend, for a brief time at least, round-tables in which topics outside your realm of interest are being discussed.

Just as there are specialized literary organizations, so are there specialized workshops for those concentrating in one particular field. The Society of Children's Book Writers, the Mystery Writers of America, the Outdoor Writers Association of America and the Western Writers of America are some of the organizations that sponsor specialized workshops.

You should consider joining a local writers' group. Meeting and communicating with fellow writers can be both a learning experience and a morale booster. Members of most of these clubs read each other's material and criticize it, which can be a valuable asset if the critic is properly qualified. Whether the group you choose is the right one can be determined only by the trial-and-error method. Should you feel it is not of value, don't hesitate to quit. Your time is too valuable to waste on a social gathering, if that is what your club turns out to be.

National writers' organizations also provide valuable services, such as assisting you in answering questions or solving problems that may arise, newsletters to keep you abreast of changes in the literary world, and market news to keep you informed about magazines and book publishers looking for writers. Select the organization carefully, making sure you understand what you are going to receive for your dues. Some associations are broad based, with members involved in all areas of writing, such as The National Writers Club and The Authors' Guild. Others, the best-known being the American Society of Journalists and Authors, concentrate on non-fiction. Several emphasize particular genres—mystery writing, science fiction, juvenile writing, Westerns, etc. Most of these require that you have a record of publication with at least a partial amount of your income derived from your writing activities. You will find brief descriptions, requirements, and amount of dues listed in the *Writer's Handbook* and *Literary Market Place*.

One advantage of joining a national writers' organization is that you are supporting your newly chosen profession. Often these associations combine their efforts to improve the lot of the freelancer by fighting for higher rates, payment on acceptance and more equitable contracts, or waging battles to obtain legislation that will be beneficial to writers. For example, largely through the efforts of The Authors' Guild, with cooperation from other organizations, a new copyright law was passed and became effective in 1978, eliminating many of the shortcomings of the previous law which had been in effect since 1906. One of the more significant changes: Previously, an author's material could not be copyrighted until after it had been published, putting the writer at the mercy of the publisher. The new law grants the copyright to the author at the moment of creation. This is only one of many projects and causes promoted by writers' organizations, and support of your profession is as vital as a doctor's support of the American Medical Association.

Another element in your curriculum consists of homework. You should not only read the masters, the greats in literature, but study them assiduously. Read Ernest Hemingway's works for examples of clarity and powerful prose. Boswell's works are a prime illustration of the importance of details, of the trivial. For elegance of style, select any of Walter Pater's books. Charles Dickens' books provide the best role models for developing characterization.

To imitate their words or ideas is not the purpose of your study. You should analyze their methods and constantly ask yourself why their creations have such enduring value. In all of your reading, look for particular mannerisms and favorite words. Note the sentence structure. Does the author have a particular technique he uses to avoid a monotony of style? How does he handle transition? How does he get characters from one scene to another? Especially analyze the opening paragraphs of the book or story, and the beginning of each chapter as well. After finishing a book, review it in your mind and try to discover why (or if) the author was successful in achieving his objective.

Read avidly the technical books on writing, with emphasis on those that are related to the field of writing you have decided upon. If you are primarily interested in the novel, some of the better reference works are Lawrence Block's *Writing the Novel; From Plot to Print; Structuring Your Novel: From Basic Idea to Finished Manuscript*, by Robert Meredith and John D. Fitzgerald; *An Autobiography*, by Anthony Trollope; and *The Story of a Novel*, by Thomas Wolfe.

For the short story writer, I recommend Hallie Burnett's *On Writing the Short Story;* Whit Burnett's *The Modern Short Story in the Making;* William Samson's *The Birth of a Story;* and Louise Boggess's *How to Write Short Stories that Sell.*

Three excellent books on writing for children are *Writing*

Juvenile Stories and Novels: How to Write and Sell Fiction for Young People, by Phyllis Whitney; *Writing for Children and Teenagers*, by Jane Andrews Wyndham; and *Writing Books for Children*, by Jane H. Yolen.

For general books on fiction technique, some of the best include Bernard DeVoto's *The World of Fiction;* John Gardner's *The Art of Fiction: Note on Craft for Young Writers;* John Kuehl's *Write and Rewrite: A Study of the Creative Process;* Jean Z. Owen's *Professional Fiction Writing: A Practical Guide to Modern Techniques.*

I urge you to accumulate a collection of classic works and surround yourself with important books. By building such an atmosphere in which to work, you may find your own writing enhanced through mental osmosis. If you own these books, instead of obtaining them through the library or borrowing them from friends, you are free to make comments in the margins or highlight certain passages. In my reading, I use the blank pages in the back of a book to indicate portions containing material I may wish to refer to, along with a brief notation as to why they are important to me.

In addition to the works of the masters, your library should include some basic reference works. Listed here are my personal choices for books every writer should own:

Dictionaries:

> *Random House College Dictionary* (published by Random House. 170,000 entries). Abridged.
>
> *Webster's Ninth New Collegiate Dictionary* (published by Merriam-Webster. 160,000 entries). Abridged.

The two basic forms of dictionaries are abridged and unabridged. Unabridged dictionaries contain virtually all the words in the English language; however, they are revised less frequently than abridged editions. Most professional writers prefer an abridged edition, and one that has been revised in the past four years. Merely looking at the copyright date in a dictionary does not indicate when it was last revised, only when it was last printed. Normally the publisher will indicate on the copyright page the year of the last revision.

Encyclopedias: A good set of encyclopedias will save the writer innumerable trips to the library and often the expense of making photocopies of various items needed in researching a book or an article. Unfortunately, encyclopedias do go out of date rather quickly; obtaining yearly updates, if available, is recommended. The two best-known sets are the *Brittanica* and the *Americana*. For a one-volume set, the *Columbia Encyclopdedia* is fairly complete, with brief, unsigned articles and illustrations limited to maps.

Grammar and Usage:

The Elements of Style, by Strunk and White. One of the most concise, and perhaps the best book ever written on the correct use of words.

Write Right, by Jan Venolia. A simplified, easy-to-use grammar book.

Word Books:

Webster's New Dictionary of Synonyms (Merriam-Webster)

Roget's Thesaurus of English Words and Phrases (St. Martin's Press). Valuable handbook of synonyms and near synonyms; helps select the precise word.

Bartlett's Familiar Quotations (Little Brown and Company). The most comprehensive book of quotations ever published.

Bibliographies:

The Writer's Advisor (published by Gale Research Company). Includes 4,259 listings of books and articles covering all facets of writing.

Fact Books:

The World Almanac (published annually by the Newspaper Enterprise Association).

Your reference materials should include a subscription to *The Writer* or *Writer's Digest,* preferably both, and these should be a part of your required reading. One phase of my routine is reviewing all of the articles and maintaining a clip file of those important to my work. Today, with the advent of the word processor, I enter on a disk the titles and a brief summary of pertinent material, along with the date of the issue for future reference. Typical of the contents are such subjects as, "How to Write a Novel," "The Hook and Eye Appeal" (how to write article openings that catch and hold the reader), "The Poet's Workshop," "Historical and Modern Romances," "Confessions of a Novelist," "Turning Experience into Fiction," etc.

Both of these magazines are also excellent sources for market information, as well as for ideas, which will be discussed more in detail in Keys Number Four and Number Nine.

Now that you have assembled all of the tools, it's time to indulge in some mental exercises, to pump iron as the muscle-builders say. A writer's success may be measured in direct ratio to his powers of observation, powers that can be increased through persistent practice.

Perhaps one of the best books focusing on mental exercise is Dorothea Brande's *Becoming a Writer*. She suggests that one must see oneself objectively: "Get up and go through a door. From the moment you stand on the threshold, turn yourself into your own object of attention. What do you look like, standing there? How do you walk?"

Take a stroll down an unfamiliar street, then stop and write your impressions in your notebook. Be as detailed as possible. What were the houses like? What about people you saw? Were there children playing in the park? Recapture your image of the trees, the shrubs, the lawns and the street lights. Remember the sounds you may have heard—traffic noises on the street, dogs barking, or children crying. Every few weeks repeat this exercise in a different part of town. And do things you would not ordinarily do, such as visiting a museum or attending a home show, an exhibition, or an art gallery.

I referred earlier to the importance of tapping your unconscious mind as a possible springboard, a starting point, when you first go to your typewriter. Brande suggests that you arise a half hour early each morning and, before turning on the TV or reading the morning paper, before talking to anyone, write randomly about anything that pops into your head. It may be a series of random, unrelated ideas, a strange dream or a recollection out of the past. Continuing this exercise over a period of time will enable you to use your unconscious mind, giving a spontaneous rhythm to your creative efforts. File the results of your subliminal writing away, occasionally rereading your efforts. Often you may find a priceless gem that you will be able to expand into a short story, an article, or a novel. Most assuredly you will learn more about yourself in this searching of your mind.

Some other reference works that relate to your psychological approach to writing are Gabriele L. Rico's *Writing the Natural Way: Using Right Brain Techniques to Release Your Expressive Powers*, and *If You Want to Write*, by Brenda Ueland.

Finally, your preparation to be a writer must involve the willingness to sacrifice, to put writing ahead of other activities, such as cocktail parties, golf, fishing, the theatre, television, and the opera. There are times when such outside pleasures are necessary, but they must be planned to serve a purpose. In *The Summing Up*, Somerset Maugham advised that "the writer can only be fertile if he renews himself and he can only renew himself if his soul is constantly enriched by fresh experience."

Unless you understand that the emotional drives required for your writing are the same as those that you deal with in your daily life, you will find your writing a difficult, if not impossible, task. The major problem of a beginning writer is a lack of purpose, a searching for a defined field, the particular genre or form in which he can best communicate. In simple terms, he doesn't know what he wants to write about. He wants guidelines, but unfortunately in the early stages he cannot have them. In the beginning his writing is experimental and exploratory, not unlike the scientist searching for a cure for cancer. The author should write about anything that comes into his head, continuing his search for the expression that will not only provide satisfaction in his own mind, but will supply the means for communicating to his audience.

Having surmounted these initial difficulties, you may then be faced with additional adversities. You may hear a clever remark or become involved in an incident that made such an impression that you felt a compulsion to include it in your work, even though it really doesn't belong. You should also avoid the temptation to adopt literary affectations, both in style and vocabulary, in order to impress the reader. As Jean Owens stresses in *Professional Fiction Writing*, "A professional writer must master technique so the reader finds the writing clear and easy to assimilate; he has learned not to strut in prose because this bores the reader; he has learned to sacrifice the luxury of reticence and force himself to write scenes with emotional impact because this is what the reader seeks in fiction."

Another malady that afflicts most word merchants is writer's block, which should be considered as just another challenge. You may find that some wordless recreation will provide the stimulus to get the creative juices flowing again. One writer, faced with the problem, found that playing solitaire was a prescription for her. A successful mystery writer, finding a difficult spot in his novel, would take off the afternoon and go fishing; and still another preferred horseback riding as a remedy.

There is no common solution to writer's block, and through persistence and trial and error you may find your own answer. According to Maxine Lewis in *The Magic Key to Successful Writing*, "The best way to deal with blockage—which is usually simply fear—is to face it at the start in the small blockages many writers feel whenever they sit down at the typewriter. . . . The key is to relax, to remake your decision to remind your subconscious that this is the time you had set to write, on this day." Those with the necessary convictions will overcome these temporary setbacks, and the others will fall by the wayside. Two books that offer some excellent suggestions to overcome this dilemma are Mike Rose's *Writer's Block: The Cognitive Dimension*, and Victoria Nelson's *Writer's Block and How to Use It*.

Elliot Blackston, one of the more successful short story writers of a few decades ago, gave this advice: "After he has come to acknowledge that . . . writing is a serious business . . . and to believe he can make a substantial success of it by hard work, plenty of time and unfailing energy, then it remains only for him to fortify himself with full confidence, and let nothing divert him from the course he has planned."

Key Four

Developing Your Idea Factory

All of the preparation, exercises and classes you attend, books you read and workshops you visit are unproductive if you have nothing worthwhile about which to write. Shakespeare said, "The play's the thing." The author says, "The idea's the thing." Seeking fresh, original subjects or new approaches to current topics are challenges facing the creative writer.

The issue may not be world-shaking, or the problem of such magnitude that it will change the course of history. Large or small, your ideas should serve a purpose: to instruct, to entertain, to amuse, to improve the reader's outlook or to challenge. You might write a treatise concerning the controversy over nuclear weapons, an article about raising children or how to improve your neighborhood parks. If you are writing a novel, its scope can be as universal as Tolstoy's *War and Peace,* or as limited as Betty MacDonald's *A Tree Grows in Brooklyn,* or a folksy book like Garrison Kellior's *Lake Wobegon Days,* or an entertaining spy thriller like Clive Cussler's *Cyclops.*

In the several thousand manuscripts I've read over the past thirty years, the flaw I've found occurring most frequently is a lack of freshness and originality. The novels sound like leftovers from Sunday's pot roast, and not nearly as tasty as the first time around. Articles, likewise, treat subjects that have been beaten into the ground, too often a collection of material gleaned from other magazines, with little, if any, creativity on the part of the author. By using your own experiences and knowledge, plus extensive research of primary sources, not only will your story have a unique quality, but will impart to the reader excitement, emotional involvement and a feeling of satisfaction. When the reader comes to the end, he should feel that the author has been honest and sincere, and has come to a logical conclusion.

Max Gunther was asked: "What does a good idea feel like?" He answered, "It feels big, an idea that has relevance to the lives of many people." It should also be something you feel strongly about, and that, in one way or another, will satisfy the reader. Is it worth the days, weeks, or months of work you are going to put into it?

How do you come up with imaginative, original ideas? Where do you find them? I've mentioned previously the need for drawing upon your own experiences, occupation, education and hobbies. Literary agent Scott Meredith suggests that "if you know a man who is unhappy because his wife is so extravagant that she spends more money on her own clothing than the upkeep of her children," you may have the germ of a story idea. "This doesn't mean, when you're settling down to write a story, that it will necessarily be about a man whose wife is extravagant. . . . It is the basic causes behind these cases which are important to you. . . . Every human problem of which you are aware can be transmuted into a dozen different story ideas."

Whenever you make a new acquaintance, you may have the subject for a story or an article if you make a conscious effort to seek out the details of his or her life. On a particular day, should you talk to ten different people, you may have ten new ideas. Be a good listener and a good observer. Keep constantly in mind that you are searching for article ideas or plots for your short story or novel.

Scanning the daily newspapers or weekly news magazines for unusual items should be a part of your routine. Don't confine your reading to the front page headlines. You'll often find a golden nugget in a brief item buried on page 23. And don't overlook the personal columns, since typical entries relate to personal problems: offers of romance, warnings to estranged lovers or notices for runaways to return home. The lost and found columns can be an excellent source, a springboard to a broader article on unusual items that are lost at football games, on airplanes and in restaurants.

A visit to your library can provide you with an unlimited number of topics. The *Reader's Guide to Periodicals*, trade journals, newsletters, directories and government abstracts are just a few of the reference works at your fingertips.

Maintain a file of clippings, organizing them into categories that, while not meaningful to others, suit your own purposes. I have over 200 separate file folders, all filled with clippings. A few of the labels are:

Propaganda
The Nature of Mankind
Civil Rights
Labor Unions
Political Campaigns
Local Governments
The Space Age
Education and Youth
The State of Morality
Censorship
"How to" Travel Ideas
The War on Noise
The Drinking American
Book Ideas
"What If" Story Ideas
Illiteracy
Ghost Towns
Unusual Personalities

Some writers prefer to use 9″ x 12″ envelopes with descriptive labels, instead of file folders. Select the system that works best for you. Regardless of the method, you should set up a card file as a cross reference or, if you use a word processor, enter the subjects on a disk, including brief notes relating to each.

You will discover unlimited raw material for your idea factory as you begin your research expedition. It is through searching and researching that you broaden your horizons, develop expertise in new areas, and increase your scope as a writer. For example, if you are planning an article on the history of railroading, you might start by referring to the *Reader's Guide to Periodical Literature* under the subject heading of "Railroads." In the process, you may encounter a dozen or more stories relating to various adventures connected to railroading, from the earliest days to Amtrak.

Creative people too often consider research a boring, distasteful part of their writing career. Unfortunately, this attitude leads to superficial, sloppily done, inaccurate reporting. One should compare doing research with building the foundation of a house. If the footings aren't deep enough or the concrete isn't allowed sufficient time to dry properly, the home will soon deteriorate and your dream castle will turn into a haunted house.

Credibility is essential, whether you are writing novels or nonfiction. Rex Alan Smith, one of America's leading historians, related the story at a writers' workshop of an author who wrote an account of Custer's Last Stand, stating that the day of the battle was bitterly cold, with a Chinook wind blowing from the West. Smith pointed out that a Chinook is a very warm wind, and that the day of the battle was unusually mild. This may seem to be an insignificant error, but it destroyed the credibility of that particular author.

Too many writers decide that they would rather write fiction for the wrong reason, using the rationale that they won't have to do research, but can merely sit at the typewriter and create from their imagination. Not true. If you read works of successful novelists, it becomes obvious that many months of intensive research preceded the actual writing of their books. James Michener, for example, has the equivalent of a library full of notes and reference works for just one project—in addition to his traveling to the sources and living among the people who are native to the region about which he is writing.

Research, like writing, requires knowledge and training. Knowing the proper methods, the correct procedures and the best sources, will make your time spent as a researcher more productive and less tedious.

Four of the most common research methods are:

1. **Interviewing:** One of the best ways to obtain primary source information. This is particularly helpful when you want to know more about the subject than you can obtain from published material.

2. **Reading:** If you know where to look, you can find

published information on virtually any subject.

3. **Observing:** One of the most important aspects, since writing from first-hand, personal experience adds credibility and authenticity to your work.

4. **Reasoning:** Assembling all of the material and your knowledge, then putting them together for the purpose of reaching a conclusion.

To obtain the maximum value from whichever methods you use, it's necessary for you to be prepared. For example, when interviewing, read beforehand as much background information about your subject as possible. If he or she has written a book, read it assiduously, noting particular passages that you might wish to bring up in the interview. This effort not only appeals to the subject's ego but gives you a basis for more productive questions, and will enable you to obtain answers that have not already appeared in print.

Listen closely for new leads. Let the interviewee do the talking, but direct the conversation so it stays on the subject. If you aren't recording the interview, transcribe your notes as soon as possible, while the interview is fresh in your mind. If you are recording, be sure that your subject has given permission to be taped.

Learning how to use the other research methods properly is just as important as learning how to conduct an interview.

Fortunately, writers have at their disposal thousands of reference sources, with much of the information available at little or no cost, the most obvious being the local public library. In addition, there are university and college libraries, historical society libraries, corporate libraries, medical, legal and other professional libraries.

The *American Library Directory* lists over 25,000 libraries in the United States and several thousand in Canada. The listing for each is complete enough that the researcher can decide if the library is sufficiently specialized in his or her subject area to visit or contact by letter or phone. Another volume, *Subject Collections: A Guide to Special Book Collections*, lists special collections of books in libraries throughout the country. The *Directory of Special Libraries and Information Centers* has more than 13,000 entries.

Getting to know your library, and your librarian, are necessities for the working writer. Spend as much time as you can in learning the library's system of filing. Becoming familiar with the Dewey Decimal Classifications, used by the Library of Congress and practically every library in the U.S., can save you hours of time. With the advent of the computer and other technological advances, it's also important to learn to use these new tools.

In your public library, the *Readers' Guide to Periodical Literature* is one of the most comprehensive sources for finding references to subjects, events and persons. It lists what articles were written by whom, about what, in what publication and when. The Guide starts with 1900, and includes several hundred (but not all) magazines published from 1900 until the present. A secondary benefit when using the Guide is that it will stimulate and expand your idea factory. *Poole's Guide to Periodical Literature* includes publications which may not be in the Reader's Guide, and you will also find other, more specialized guides that can be helpful in providing supplemental sources.

The *Subject Guide to Books in Print* (R.R. Bowker) is excellent for finding books needed for your research and to determine if your topic has been overworked. Bowker also publishes *Books in Print* (listings by author), and *Books in Print* (listings by title).

Some sources frequently overlooked are associations, corporations, and universities. Directories are available listing most of the associations in the United States and Canada covering every conceivable field of business, industry and commerce. Most of these associations can provide the writer with all kinds of information about their particular area of interest.

Likewise, experts with various specialties are readily available for interviews, to verify facts or to write introductions to books. The Nonfiction Writers of America publishes the *Media Contacts Guide & Telephone Directory* listing experts in everything from Aging to Ulcers. The University of Denver publishes a comprehensive Experts List, most of these offering their expertise at no cost to the writer. Other universities provide similar services that will add authenticity to your writing project.

The United States government is an invaluable source of research materials. To determine the branch you should contact, refer to the *U.S. Government Organization Manual*, which lists the purpose of every government agency. Once you have determined the proper agency, send a request for information to the Public Information Office of that agency.

You have probably heard historians refer to 'primary' and 'secondary' sources. A primary source relates to information or material not previously published. It could be a diary, an interview, or an unpublished manuscript. A secondary source would be material that has been previously published. Obviously the more primary source material you use, the more valuable your work becomes. Again the U.S. Government can be of help, since the Library of Congress publishes the *National Union Catalog of Manuscripts*. *A Guide to Archives and Manuscripts in the United States*, published by Yale University Press also provides a listing of primary source material. *Oral History in the United States—A Directory* is another reference listing unpublished material (published by Columbia University).

Over 16,000 publications are available from the U.S. Government Printing Office. Catalogs listing all of the titles are published at frequent intervals and are available at your library or by writing the GPO.

Another source for reference material on a world-wide basis is the United Nations. Thousands of books are available through the UN, and catalogs listing the titles can be obtained for the asking.

In your research, you may encounter books mentioned that are no longer in print, but that may include valuable information for your project. Many of these are available on microfilm through University Microfilms International, Books on Demand program, Xerox subsidiary.

Newspaper accounts of events that may have occurred many years ago often provide first-hand accounts of these happenings, but old newspapers are hard to find. Fortunately, *The New York Times* is on microfilm in most public libraries, as well as the *New York Times Index*. Likewise, the *Wall Street Journal Index* is available on microfilm.

Two books that will make your researching easier are: *Finding*

Facts Fast, by Alden Todd (Ten Speed Press), which includes excellent listings of various reference books with pertinent information about each; and *The Modern Researcher*, by Jacques Barzun and Henry F. Graf (Harcourt Brace Jovanovich), which includes an extensive bibliography of books on research. For one of the most complete bibliographies of books on writing, refer to *The Writer's Advisor*, compiled by Leland G. Alkire, Jr., and published by Gale Research Company. This guide covers books and articles about writing novels, short stories, poetry, dramatic scripts, screenplays, magazine articles, biographies, and more. Not only does it list the titles but provides a brief description concerning each source.

One habit you should develop is keeping a careful record of the source of your material. This is particularly important if you are making notes or copying passages from copyrighted material. Publishers usually (if not always) require both verification of your facts and evidence of permission to use quoted passages from copyrighted works. The proper procedure is to list the title of the book or article, the author, the particular edition you are using (First Edition, Second Edition, etc.), the date of the edition, the name of the publisher, and the page number on which the passage appears. Not only does such a record save you time should you wish to refer to the material at a later date, but it also simplifies the procedure for requesting permission to use the material.

Other reference aids you will find useful as you continue your writing career include the *World Almanac*, *Bartlett's Familiar Quotations*, and the *Great Treasury of Western Thought*, edited by Mortimer J. Adler and Charles Van Doren and published by R.R. Bowker Co. In addition to the well-known Roget's *Thesaurus*, there are many other word books of synonyms, antonyms, American slang, rhymes, foreign words and phrases. Atlases and maps are indispensable to many writers who need to be certain of geographic locations, as well as street names and points of interest in various cities. Whether it is a novel or a nonfiction history book, nothing destroys credibility in a reader's mind more quickly than discovering that the author has erroneously stated that the Snake River runs through Little Rock, or that Grand Central Park is in the Bronx.

One final quality a writer must have, in addition to ideas and research capabilities, is imagination. Whether you are writing fiction, nonfiction, poetry, or plays, imagination is an essential ingredient. David Raffelock, in a handbook entitled *The Creative Ability Developer*, divided imagination into three different categories. "Functional Imagination" he defined as the simplest kind, the ability to visualize a completed task, something as fundamental as what the lawn would look like after it has been mowed, or the appearance of a house after it has a fresh coat of paint. Functional imagination also requires that you recognize something that needs to be done, such as a civic enterprise, a change in moral standards or an improvement in programming on television.

Second is the "Ingenious Imagination," which consists of the ability to combine existing elements to establish something different or fresh, such as observing a person and thinking of him in a completely different environment.

Finally, and most rare, is "Creative Imagination," which requires the author to invent forms or ideas not hitherto written by others. When Leonardo da Vinci described plans for a flying machine, he was not combining other people's information or facts, for in his day none existed. Another aspect of creative imagination is the ability to combine visualized logic or facts with invention. Example: A writer may visualize a period of history as a living fact and then invent characters who are made to live in this environment as fully and logically as if he had known such persons intimately in reality. A novelist such as James Michener, in *Centennial* and some of his other works, is a master at the use of this kind of creative imagination.

Closely related to creative imagination is inspiration, a fiction of the mind, a journey into the subconscious, the innermost corners of the brain. I've recently read several books by authors who insist that they were divinely inspired, that the words came from an unknown source and flowed through their fingers. It is conceivable that some exaggeration may exist in these authors' convictions, but most literary scholars agree that some of the greatest literature was born out of inspiration. Samuel Johnson insisted that the language of man was the result of inspiration. "A thousand, nay, a million of children could not invent a language . . . Inspiration seems to me to be necessary to give man the faculty of speech; to inform him that he may have speech; which I think he could no more find out without inspiration, than cows or hogs would think of such a faculty."

This intangible phenomenon called inspiration should be the by-product of your creative efforts; otherwise you may fall into the trap of being unable to write because you are not "inspired." Successful writers cannot wait for the right mood, the proper moment. Having conceived their idea, and having assembled the facts and outlined their project (on paper or in their minds), they proceed with the task at the scheduled time.

Key Five

The Technique of Writing

One of Mark Twain's memorable remarks about writing was that all the words are in the dictionary and we merely need to put them in the proper order. Typical of Twain, his comment was an over-simplification, but he does make a point.

Schopenhauer held the opinion that "authors should use common words to say uncommon things. But they do just the opposite. We find them trying to clothe their very ordinary thoughts in the most extraordinary phrases, the most far-fetched, unnatural, and out-of-the-way expressions. Their sentences perpetually stalk about on stilts."

At a workshop a few years ago, one of the editors at Harper and Row discussed the reasons most manuscripts are rejected. He emphasized the importance of simple, uncomplicated writing. To him the kiss of death was the query letter in which the author claimed to have written The Great American Novel.

I've listened to many frustrated writers complain that they have read a book or watched a TV program that didn't compare with stories they have written and that have been rejected. Why, the neophyte wants to know, do publishers and TV producers accept this inferior work? Putting aside the ego of the fledgling author and possibly an exaggerated opinion of the quality of his own creation, he may not realize that a writer's success may be attributed, not to the story he tells, but how he tells it.

Hundreds of books on writing provide formulas for plotting, developing characters and outlining. You may follow these instructions implicitly, write your story and send it to a publisher, wait impatiently for a few weeks before receiving a form rejection. You may have an original plot, a solid theme and a great idea. But it just doesn't come off. As important as your story may be, unless it captivates the reader, excites him, or arouses his emotions, the chances of its being accepted are very slim. If there is a secret formula that separates the professional writer from the amateur, it probably is the difference in style. The successful novelist, short story writer or nonfiction author have a way with words, an ability to take a subject, even a nondescript idea or plot, and present it in a way that captures and maintains the reader's interest.

Unless your writing has warmth and feeling, you cannot expect to impart these qualities to the reader. Just as it is necessary to get to know the characters in your story intimately, so it is important to get to know words. "If you don't keep in touch with your readers," say Rudolph Flesch and A.H. Lass in *The Way to Write*, "you lose them."

I've emphasized the importance of studying the masters, analyzing their works and dissecting their sentences, word by word. As an exercise, compare this difference in style: "It was a cold ride up to the mountains, and Luke didn't feel very well. There were lots of stars, because night had fallen." Thomas Wolfe wrote it this way: "The ride back into the hills with Luke was cold, dark, bleak, and desolate—the very painting of his own sick soul. Black night had come when they had reached the mountains. The stars were out, and around them the great bulk of the hills was barren, bleak, and wintry-looking." Notice the imagery and the simple words, used in a dramatic way. Succinctly, Wolfe makes the reader feel he is a part of the scene and, at the same time, arouses an emotional involvement with Luke.

Analyze this descriptive passage from Hemingway's *The Sun Also Rises:* "The bus climbed steadily up the road. The country was barren and rocks stuck up through the clay. There was no grass beside the road. Looking back we could see the country spread out below. Far back the fields were squares of green and brown on the hillsides. Making the horizons were the brown mountains. They were strangely shaped. As we climbed higher the horizon kept changing. As the bus ground slowly up the road we could see other mountains coming up in the south. Then the road came over the crest, flattened out, and went into a forest. It was a forest of cork oaks, and the sun came through the trees in patches, and there were cattle grazing back in the trees. We went through the forest and the road came out and turned along a rise of land, and out ahead of us was a rolling green plain, with dark mountains beyond it. These were not like the brown, heatbaked mountains we had left behind. These were wooded and there were clouds coming down from them. The green plain stretched off. It was cut by fences and the white of the road showed through the trunks of a double line of trees that crossed the plain toward the north. As we came to the edge of the rise we saw the red roofs and white houses of Burguete ahead strung out on the plain, and away off on the shoulder of the first dark mountain was the gray metal-sheathed roof of the monastery of Roncesvalles."

In your analysis, count the number of color words Hemingway uses, and the number of single syllable words. How many simple sentences (one independent clause) does he use? Notice how he varies the length of his sentences. We should not try to imitate other writers (especially Hemingway), but learn from them. For practice, write a descriptive passage of your own of a bus ride you may have taken, or a trip on a train, or a hike in the woods, keeping in mind some of Hemingway's techniques.

One of the most important books on style is also one of the smallest—only 78 pages. It is Strunk and White's *The Elements of Style*. As E.B. White says in the introduction, "Vigorous writing is concise. A sentence should contain no unnecessary words, a paragraph no unnecessary sentences, for the same reason that a drawing should have no unnecessary lines and a machine no unnecessary parts. This requires not that the writer make all his sentences short, or that he avoid all detail and treat his subjects only in outline, but that every word tell."

The new writer often has a tendency to show off his skills, to let the reader know that he is an author, consequently interfering with the story he has to tell. Keep yourself in the background, and let your characters do the talking.

Second, avoid writing to impress the reader with your great

store of knowledge. Write naturally, using your innate abilities. Don't over-extend yourself by trying too hard. A thesaurus is an essential aid, but you should not write, especially your initial drafts, with one at your side. Not only does this slow down the creative flow; it will also make your writing sound stilted, unnatural and usually difficult to understand.

The beginning writer has a tendency to lean too heavily on adjectives and adverbs, ignoring the principle that good writing depends on nouns and verbs. Prime examples of this misuse of adverbs frequently occur in dialogue. "I hate you," he said *angrily*, or "You're a wonderful person," she said, *smiling sweetly*. In well done dialogue, the situation and the character's words and action should be adequate. Using adverbs and adjectives as crutches indicates a weakness in the author's ability to 'show', not 'tell'.

Leon Surmelian, in *Techniques of Fiction Writing*, suggests that a writer "can strengthen his style by increasing the proportion of short Saxon words in his stories. . . . Saxon words make prose concrete and energetic." He defines Saxon words as those denoting peasant strength; and Latin words, elegance. Use Saxon words for sensations and Latin words for concepts; use Saxon words for the concrete and specific, and Latin words for the abstract and general.

Whenever possible, present your story in terms that appeal to the senses: sight, hearing, smell, touch and taste. Instead of 'dog', use 'Dalmation'; instead of 'animal', use 'elephant'; instead of 'house', use 'bungalow'; instead of 'boat', use 'clipper ship' or 'schooner'. These are visual nouns that convey pictorial images.

Verbs, likewise, should be active, colorful and vivid. Instead of saying, "Joe sat in a chair," it is more effective to say, "Joe slumped in the chair." How much more meaningful it is if, instead of writing, "The thief turned into a side street to avoid the police," you say, "The bank robber careened his van around the corner, wheels screeching, as the police car closed in on him."

Another weakness that must be avoided, particularly in this day of fast-moving cars, supersonic jets, and 30-minute TV dramas, is overwriting. The writer must tell the reader what he has to know, but should not burden him with details that have little relationship to the plot. I've read many manuscripts in which several pages are devoted to something as inconsequential as a man and a woman drinking a cup of coffee. "Do you want sugar?" she asks. "Yes," he says. "How many lumps?" she inquires. "Two," he replies. "Do you prefer cream?" she remarks. And so forth.

Writers who have a particular area of expertise often will expound for pages, describing minor details about sailing a boat, flying an airplane, repairing a lawnmower or how to pitch a tent. I recently read a novel manuscript by a doctor who devoted an entire chapter to the technical aspects of an ear operation, an event that had nothing to contribute to the movement of the story.

Allow the reader to use his imagination rather than burden him with a roadblock of details. Today's stories books must move swiftly. When describing characters, for example, it's unnecessary to provide pages of description explaining what he or she is wearing or minute items concerning the character's physical appearance. Leon Uris, in *Queen's Bench System*, mentions merely that the hero had an eye patch, and left the rest of the description to the reader's imagination.

Strunk and White call the use of qualifiers, such as *rather*, *very*, *little*, *pretty*, "the leeches that infest the pond of prose, sucking the blood of words." Search for meaningful expressions and phrases, colorful words that convey images to the reader. At the same time, use figures of speech, such as similes and metaphors, sparingly, and do not mix them up. Don't start out with an apple tree and end with a watermelon patch.

Above all, write clearly, using language and sentences that can be easily understood. James P. White and Janice L. White have devoted an entire volume to *Clarity: A Text on Writing*, including many excellent excerpts from successful writers who have mastered the art of writing clearly. Strunk and White state the case emphatically: "Clarity, clarity, clarity. When you become hopelessly mired in a sentence, it is best to start fresh; do not try to fight your way through against the terrible odds of syntax. Usually what is wrong is that the construction has become too involved at some point; the sentence needs to be broken apart and replaced by two or more shorter sentences."

One clue a writer should look for that leads to obscurity is whether the writing is loaded with generalizations instead of specifics. If the language is flowery and blooming with polysyllabic words, when the sentences are filled with conjunctions, dangling participles, and subjunctive phrases, specificity and clarity disappear. The reader becomes lost in the maze.

Another ingredient in the recipe for clear writing is the use of the correct word, the exact word. A thesaurus provides you with extensive lists of words that are similar in meaning, and by studying all of the synonyms you will be able to select the one particular word that says exactly what you want to convey to the reader.

Many books are available containing lists of words often misused or misspelled, and one of these should be a part of your reference library. Here are a few examples of right and wrong words:

Accept/Except
Adopt/Adapt
Affect/Effect
Skim/Scan
About/Around
Aggravate/Irritate
Among/Between
Allusion/Illusion
Bring/Take
Lie/Lay
Capital/Capitol
Apt/Likely
Complement/Compliment
Council/Counsel
Continual/Continuous
Famous/Notorious
Less/Fewer
Good/Well
Immigrate/Emigrate
Ingenious/Ingenuous
Persecute/Prosecute
Precede/Proceed
Rise/Raise

Sit/Set

Stationary/Stationery

Each of these sets of words has a completely different meaning, but is frequently used for the other interchangeably and incorrectly. Refer to your dictionary or your thesaurus for the exact definitions and proper use. As Mark Twain said, the difference between the right and wrong word is the same as the difference between lightning and a lightning bug.

We've covered most of the basic elements of style—how to develop it and its importance to your success as a writer—but in a general way. Whether you are writing fiction, nonfiction, drama, or poetry, the elements we've discussed are essential staples.

However, as with any recipe, the seasonings can make a difference. Writing style for the novelist involves techniques that may place strong emphasis on character development, description and narrative. The dramatist is concerned with scenes and dialogue, and the historian stresses accuracy and the course of events. The poet is a master of brevity, imagery and of the sound as well as the meaning of his words.

Key Six discusses in detail the variety of writing areas available to you and how to determine which may be best suited to your skills. For now, we'll highlight some of the different aspects of style applicable to these various forms.

In fiction writing, your words must impart emotion and your scenes must be vividly described. You must overcome the temptation to overwrite. In Walter Campbell's classic book, *Professional Writing*, he says: "In narrative, one must choose the significant movement, the significant gesture; in description, one must choose the significant sensation; in exposition, one must choose the significant fact or idea; in dialogue, one must choose the significant word; in characterization, one must choose the significant motive."

To summarize, avoid the use of 'say-nothing' words. Prepositions, adverbs, conjunctions and articles generally add little to a sentence. For example, instead of "The boy went to the grocery store in order to get some candy," say, "The boy went to the grocery store to get some candy." Other useless words used frequently are "however," "nevertheless," "of course," "on the other hand," "basically," and "fundamentally."

Stick to direct statements by using active verbs, and beware of qualifying phrases. Note how the following paragraph is improved through careful editing: "Undoubtedly, limited strikes by automobile workers, if made to protest a reduction in wages and benefits, might have some effect if the demands are reasonable. If, however, these demands are carried to extremes, something which frequently happens in these cases, they would in all probability be denied and, in the long run, result in failure for the workers."

Here is the edited version: "Limited strikes—if the demands are reasonable—normally would result in increased benefits for the workers. But in strikes carried to extremes, management would fight back and in the long run, defeat the union's purpose."

The poet should resist the temptation to fill his verse with archaic expressions or unusual words that he may consider 'poetic'. He should, rather, use a living vocabulary, not unlike the words we normally find in everyday conversation. The argument that Shelley, Keats, Chaucer, and Shakespeare wrote obscure and antiquated phrases is an invalid conclusion, since in those time periods their writings were contemporary and a part of the average person's vocabulary.

More than in any other literary form, the poet must find words that are alive and meaningful, conveying images. In today's world of poetry, the thesaurus is more important than the rhyming dictionary. Instead of using a plain word like 'say,' consider these possibilities: affirm, answer, speak up, utter, suppose. Instead of 'nice', which is meaningless, select: attentive, meticulous, fastidious, tasteful, discriminating, pleasant. Some synonyms for the innocuous 'want' are: lack, deficiency, shortage, shortfall, defectiveness.

Until the emergence of Walt Whitman, poetry adhered to specific forms—there were sonnets with a specific number of lines, and poems that required rhymes and rhythm. But with a new freedom of lifestyle, poetry has achieved a greater freedom of form, with free verse a more popular version of this art than ever before. Too many would-be poets select free verse as a format, thinking that it is easy, merely rearranging prose so that it looks like a poem. Anyone serious about creating poetry should start by writing in a variety of meters. If you can write only free verse, you are apt to be cut off from the great poetry of the past. Dick Allen, in an essay entitled, "Passion and the Modern Poet," states that "the poet who cannot write a decent rhymed poem is not one to be trusted as solidly grounded in the art."

Nonfiction writing, like poetry, has evolved in style over the years. Gone is the popularity of the essay, in which the author proclaimed his philosophy, thoughts and ideas about the world in general. Today the author of nonfiction articles and books has developed a close relationship to the novelist. Successful nonfiction writing now requires an emotional involvement with characters and events as a part of the factual material the author is trying to impart to the reader. A few decades ago, all that was required of the nonfiction writer was adequate research and well-organized material, with a premise and a satisfying conclusion. The modern reader demands the same criteria of style he seeks in a novel, with a liberal use of anecdotes and fully developed characters with whom he can identify. The emphasis must concentrate on the people involved in the event, rather than on the event itself. As Aristotle proclaimed, "It is not enough to know what to say; we must also say it in the right way."

As with the novelist, the nonfiction writer's work should sparkle and have a certain rhythm, at the same time having the elements of clarity and simplicity. Sentences should be short and uncomplicated, and the writer's vocabulary should be understandable and exact. The nonfiction writer must excite the reader and challenge, satisfy, entertain and educate him.

The dramatist, compared with writers of all other kinds of literature, is the least concerned with style. How he describes a scene and the action is seldom read by anyone other than the director, the producer, or the actors. A dramatist's style is reflected in the dialogue, the words the actors speak and how they perform the scene. The author, on the other hand, must have the capability of visualizing and accurately describing the setting, of detailing in his mind all of the minute items essential to a successful production.

These are the variations of style, each individualized to the particular area of writing you may select. But the basic elements are common to all. As Maxine Lewis writes in *The Magic Key to Successful Writing:* "The writer . . . in developing his material, is not clothing his feelings and ideas with words, but is trying *to bring out of imaginative resource the words that are clothed with feeling and drenched with the ideas he wishes to express.* This is his key to individual style and to becoming verbally articulate."

Key Six

A Time for Decision

From early childhood through your adult years, you are constantly required to make decisions, some quite simple and others much more difficult. As a youngster, you were faced with selecting games to play. During your elementary school days, your parents may have given you the choice of taking piano or clarinet lessons. In high school there were electives— geometry or German, typing or shorthand, home economics or manual training. If you attended college, it was necessary to make more important decisions. You had to select your major and your minor subjects, studies that might have a vital impact on the rest of your life.

Once again, it's decision-making time. One of the questions frequently asked at workshops is: "What should I write about?" The options are many and quite often your initial choice may change as you develop in your career. You may start by writing short articles or fillers, or poetry, eventually moving into a career as a novelist, a historian, a dramatist.

Let's examine some of the possibilities:

Articles:
> How-to; Self-help; Editorial; Political; Inspirational; Travel; Technical; Business; Book Reviews; Humor; Trade Journals; Essays.

Poetry and Verse:
> Free Verse; Sonnets; Ballads; Haiku; Experimental; Classical; Dramatic; Greeting Cards; Songs.

Drama and Musical Theatre:
> Broadway Plays; Little Theatre; Educational Theatre;

Movies; TV Dramas; Musical Comedies.

Novels:

Detective, Mystery, Spy and Intrigue; Contemporary Romance; Gothic Romance; Science Fiction, Fantasy, Horror; Historical; Inspirational; Children and Young Adult; Mainstream; Experimental.

Short Stories:

Contemporary; Romance; Family; Science Fiction, Mystery, Fantasy, Horror; Humor; Experimental; Historical; Children's, Young Adult. Short short stories.

Nonfiction Books:

Biography; Autobiograpy; History; Travel; Inspirational; Philosophy; Textbooks; How-to; Self-Help; Technical.

Other opportunities also exist. As a journalist, you may be intrigued by the field of investigative reporting, or you may choose as a starting point being a stringer for a newspaper or a magazine, or copywriting for an advertising agency or a public relations firm. Speechwriting for politicians or executives can be a profitable way to go. You can become an editor for a house organ or a technical writer for a large corporation, or you may decide to be a ghostwriter, or specialize in writing company histories or hire yourself out to organizations to write annual reports.

How do you make the decision as to the kind of writing you wish to do? Here are some questions that may help you make choices:

1. What do you like to read?
2. What activities are you most interested in?
3. In what areas are you the most knowledgeable?
4. What kind of educational background do you have?
5. What goals do you have in your writing career?

Consider each of the major categories listed at the beginning of Key Six and determine which of them seems best suited to your talents.

Articles:

1. Ingenuity in getting ideas.
2. An intuition as to what would interest readers.
3. An ability to plan logically and present ideas in an orderly way.

4. Can you expand your ideas into an outline?
5. Are you a competent researcher?
6. Do you enjoy interviewing people?
7. Are you competent at taking notes?
8. Do you have skill in writing lucidly, in using the exact word?
9. Can you devise an interest-arousing beginning?
10. Are you adept at including anecdotal material in your articles?

Poetry, Verse, Songs:

1. Do you have a feeling for the rhythm of words?
2. Are you knowledgeable about verse forms?
3. Do you have fresh, original ideas?
4. Are you able to create vivid images?
5. Do you have something meaningful to say that can be said only through poetry?
6. Do you enjoy reading poetry?
7. Do you have a knack for using metaphors and similes?
8. Do you have strong emotional feelings about specific things?
9. Do you have a sense of the particular, as opposed to the general?

Poetry offers a minimum of financial rewards unless you happen to have extraordinary talent and a considerable amount of luck. If you have chosen poetry as your primary interest, you should ask yourself why you've made the selection. Clement Wood, in *Poet's Handbook*, offers some reasons:

"1. Because you want the social grace of being able to play your part in games requiring versification, as well as the ability to write acceptable verses on such occasions as a birthday, anniversary, etc.

2. Because you want to round out your powers of self-expression.

3. Because you want to increase your prestige by being known as a poet.

4. Because you want to add to your income by the use of versification, whether from winning last line limerick contests, writing and selling greeting card mottoes, or for special magazine markets, or song lyrics or poems having wide enough appeal

to have sales value."

Drama and Musical Theatre:

1. Do you have these requirements?
   a. A knowledge of the stage.
   b. Comprehension of the limitations of the stage.
   c. Understanding of the format of scriptwriting.
2. Are you able to create believable characters through dialogue and action?
3. Can you develop conversation that is natural and necessary to move the plot along?
4. Are you able to differentiate your characters through their speech?
5. Can you create characters who have a sympathetic impact on the audience?
6. Do you have the ability to create conflict?
7. Do you have something important to say?

The Novel:

These are some of the requirements you need to be a successful novelist:

1. Determination to make time available for your writing when outside pressures become demanding.
2. Maintaining continuous enthusiasm and determination, regardless of unforeseen commitments to other projects.
3. Gaining sustenance, courage and inspiration from what you are writing every day.
4. Selection of a subject that is fresh, important, or entertaining.
5. The ability to use your powers of observation.
6. The avoidance of the common pitfalls: useless wordage, flowery language, unnecessary descriptions, pointless characterizations.
7. A knowledge of the facts and circumstances required to make your story believable.
8. Understanding your characters fully so that the reader is concerned about what happens to them.

Writing for Children:

1. Do you understand the hopes and ideals of children, their likes and dislikes?
2. Can you write on a children's level without writing down to them?

3. Does the main character have an appeal to children, and does he/she solve his/her own problems?
4. Does your story have a theme that is meaningful without preaching?
5. Can you write about children's problems in terms that they can understand and accept?
6. Can you maintain interest throughout the story?
7. Are you able to use figures of speech that are understandable and acceptable for young people?
8. Can you maintain the illusion of reality?

Short Stories:

A successful short story writer should have these qualifications:

1. The ability to get your story off to a fast start, to create the illusion of reality immediately.
2. Clear, concise writing, using simple action words.
3. Talent to develop ingenious, fresh plots.
4. The capability to devise believable characters, using a minimum of descriptive details.
5. Revealing characters through action.
6. Setting the stage and stating the problem quickly, as a part of your introduction.
7. Having a thorough knowledge of the background and setting of your story.

As with the novel and most other forms of writing, you should analyze short stories currently being published. Read popular magazines as well as the literary and small publications that emphasize this form. You can also learn much from the successful craftsmen whose work appear in anthologies. *The Oxford Book of Short Stories* (Oxford University Press, 1981); *The World of the Short Story* (Houghton Mifflin, 1986), edited by Clifton Fadiman; and an older work, *The Modern Short Story in the Making* (Hawthorn Books, 1964), edited by Whit and Hallie Burnett, are excellent collections worth studying.

Non-fiction Books:

Biography

1. A strong interest in the subject.
2. Willingness to devote a long period of time in researching, interviewing.

3. An understanding of the background of the subject, his environment, his significance to the period in which he lived or lives.
4. An ability to involve the reader emotionally in the subject.
5. Selection of a subject who hasn't been written about, or new unpublished information or a different slant.
6. Selection of a subject who is a celebrity or who has made an important contribution or is unusual in some respect that makes him interesting to the reader.

History
1. Do you have a deep interest in past events?
2. Are you willing to spend hundreds of hours in researching your subject?
3. Are you an accurate taker of notes?
4. Do you have a subject that hasn't been overwritten, or do you have a source for new material?
5. Do you have a different slant that will add knowledge to the subject?
6. Are you able to be completely objective in your approach?
7. Are you willing and able to travel to obtain first-hand information?
8. Do you have the writing talent to make your historical account come to life for the reader?

Travel
1. Do you enjoy traveling?
2. When you travel, are you observant, not only of the places you visit, but of the lifestyle of the people who live there?
3. Are you able to write lively, interesting anecdotes related to your travels?
4. Can you write about people as well as places?
5. Are you sure that the subject hasn't been overdone, or that you have a different slant?
6. Do you enjoy reading travel articles and books?

How-to, Self-help
1. Do you consider yourself an expert in the subject about which you plan to write?
2. Do you know people with credentials whom you can interview about the subject?
3. Is your subject one that will offer help or guidance to readers?

4. Is the subject of wide appeal?
5. Do you have the ability to use lively anecdotes or write with a style that will hold the reader's interest?
6. Can you write in layman's terms, avoiding technical details that are unnecessary and boring to the average reader?

Textbooks

The market for textbooks is an ongoing one, with the possibility of sales continuing year after year. But the author must either be directly involved in the field of education, or have expertise as well as a reputation in the subject about which he is writing.

1. Do you have the ability to write at the level of the students for whom your book is intended?
2. Are you able to design test questions that will be usable in the classroom?
3. Is your subject one that has not been overwritten, or do you have a different slant?
4. Do you have contacts with people in the school market?
5. Can you obtain experts to review your material and write an introduction?

Once you have selected the particular field of writing which has the most appeal for you, and which you feel most qualified to pursue, you should study the necessary techniques and analyze the works of others who have been successful in that field.

In addition to the information included here, refer to *The Writer's Advisor* for a complete bibliography of books in your chosen categories.

Writing Articles

In article writing, subject and theme are the most important elements, followed by the method of presentation and finally, writing style. When choosing a subject, be as specific as possible. An article on world economics would be difficult to sell, but narrowed down to "Should America Have a Free Trade Policy?" it would have a better chance. Using as a subject, "The Japanese-American Trade War," would improve its possibilities with an editor even more.

Once you have decided upon an idea, make a rough, general outline and then do your research. If you find, as you study other books and articles on the same subject, that you can't come up with anything new or different, it is better to forget the idea rather than rehash what others have already written. But if you have a new slant, continue your research and, when complete, prepare a comprehensive outline.

Before you start to write, analyze the outline and ask: Does your subject have a theme, a point to make, and a satisfying conclusion? Put yourself in the position of the reader and try to imagine the questions he might have about the subject. When you start to write, anticipate his curiosity and give him the answers.

The lead paragraph in an article not only must set the stage, but also must make the editor eager to read on, and should provide a hint as to its direction. Many books about article writing stress the importance of starting with an anecdote. While this may be valid, the anecdote must have a direct relationship to the basic substance of the article.

The middle portion of your article should include all of the facts that sustain your conclusion. Unfortunately, it can be dull unless you develop the technique of spicing it up so it will move at a fast pace. Here the use of anecdotes can be of immeasurable help. Likewise, quotes from experts not only add authenticity, but make the factual material much easier for the reader to swallow. Other essential elements to avoid boredom are clarity, force, and that intangible factor referred to as flavor.

Make your ending brief and satisfying. Avoid summarizing the body of your article, or ending with a quote.

Once completed, read it over with some of these questions in mind: Do I have all of the facts and statistics necessary to make the point I originally had in mind? Is the material well organized, with logical transitions? Does it flow naturally? Does my conclusion answer all of the reader's questions?

Writing Poetry and Verse

In the words of Socrates, "All good poets . . . compose their beautiful poems not by art, but because they are inspired and possessed . . . For the poet is a light and winged and holy thing, and there is no invention in him until he has been inspired and is out of his senses, and the mind is no longer in him: when he has not attained to this state, he is powerless and is unable to utter his oracles."

Although poetry is the most difficult of the art forms—as well as at the bottom of the payment scale—it is the one most often attempted by the beginning writer. One reason is that we are exposed to verses from our earliest childhood. Our parents read us nursery rhymes like "Hi diddle diddle," or "Jack be nimble, Jack be quick," long before the fairytale phase. Another appealing reason is that poems can be very brief and therefore completed in a short time. And a third reason— actually a misconception—is that most poems are personal and subjective, requiring no research—just inspiration and a little imagination.

The aspiring poet who believes these falsehoods qualify him to write poetry will end up creating shallow, conventional, ordinary verses with trite, overworked themes. Unless his ego is such that he is willing to pay to have his poetry published, he will soon become discouraged as his stack of rejection slips mounts. For those who write verse for their own amusement and the therapeutic value it may have, these goals may be sufficiently satisfying to be worth the effort.

The words, poetry and verse, are often used interchangeably, but technically poetry is composed of verses, or a single verse. In today's terminology, poetry is considered a higher art form. Wordsworth called it "the spontaneous overflow of powerful feelings recollected in tranquility," Poe referred to poetry as "the rhythmical creation of beauty," and Carlyle said it is "the harmonious unison of man with nature." Here is Clement Wood's definition: "Poetry is verse which produces a deep emotional response . . . Verse is words arranged according to some conventionalized repetition."

One can be a versifier without being a poet, writing light verse in the style of Dorothy Parker or Ogden Nash, or song lyrics or greeting card messages. Opportunities for the versifier are much more golden than for the poet, but lack the prestige usually accorded to the successful writer of poetry. Unless you have a special talent for writing humor in verse, you may find markets difficult to crack. Songwriting, likewise, can be extremely competitive, with the added hazard of scams that promise you instant success for a substantial fee, but rarely deliver. Usually the amateur songwriter ends up with a very expensive, poor quality demo record and no one to play it.

On the plus side, the greeting card market is flourishing and pays well, considering the brevity of the material. In the past twenty years the number of greeting card companies has more than doubled, and the variety of subjects has similarly increased. Today, in addition to the conventional greeting card, there are juvenile, humorous, studio, inspirational and informal classifications. Within each of these classifications are the special occasions: Birthday, anniversary, graduation, Mother's Day, Father's Day, Easter, Christmas, Halloween, Thanksgiving, etc. A visit to your gift shop and a few dollars spent on buying some typical cards in these different categories will pay off if you are serious about writing for this market.

Writing Drama

Today the writing of drama can be divided into three basic categories: The theatre (stage plays), the movies, and television. For the successful playwright, a pot of gold may lie at the end of the rainbow, plus notoriety and fame. But the pot of gold is just as elusive as the rainbow. Not only is the competition fierce, but the mechanics of finding a way to have your play, script, or concept even looked at by a producer are difficult and frustrating.

I've mentioned in a previous chapter the danger of setting your goals too high, ending in discouragement and despair. This is especially true for those who aspire to write movie or TV scripts. Unless you are fortunate enough to have a contact, a friend in the business, or a legitimate agent, the chances of your script being read are remote.

The best place to start is in your own hometown. In almost all fair-sized communities you will find local theatres, or colleges that present stage productions. These are frequently experimental in nature, and are open to the novice playwright.

To obtain the experience needed to become a playwright, you should plan a relatively simple, one-act play, with a small cast of characters and a stage setting that is not overly complicated. The same basic principles apply to a one-act play as to a three-act full-blown, dramatic extravaganza, except on a more limited scale. You must have conflict—the stronger, the better. And your play must evoke emotion within the audience. As with a novel or a short story, unless the reader cares about the characters and feels a human involvement with them, he loses interest in the outcome.

Some other basic elements the scriptwriter must incorporate in his play are: Get into the action as quickly as possible and keep conversations between the characters short and meaningful. In today's market, there is no room for Shakespearian soliloquies. Finally, maintain momentum, constantly building toward your final climax. When the curtain falls, the audience should feel that the play has ended and not merely stopped.

In the field of scriptwriting, whether the play is for television or the stage, the proper format is an essential consideration, more than in any other area of writing. There are numerous books available that provide examples of the professional method of writing scripts. Again, refer to the bibliography in *The Writer's Advisor* for sources.

Two expanding markets offering opportunities for the beginning playwright are documentaries and business films. With the advent of cable television, the documentary is playing an important role. And many large corporations are willing to pay substantial fees to those who can create a professional script adaptable for closed circuit video.

Writing Novels

The novel is defined as a long work of fiction (usually a minimum of 50,000 words) that comes in many different varieties, referred to as 'genres'. These include mysteries, science fiction, historical, mainstream, gothic and contemporary romance, Western, horror, and others. Novels for children and young adults fit into most of these categories, but are generally shorter (20,000 to 30,000 words, and considerably shorter for illustrated children's books).

Regardless of the genre, all fiction has three basic characteristics: it must be imaginative; it must be based on a conflict; it must be entertaining either by virtue of what happens, the emotional quality, or the way the story is told.

With rare exceptions, a novel must have a beginning, a middle, and an end. As simplistic and fundamental as this may sound, many beginning writers fail to adhere to this basic structure. Some write stories that have a strong beginning, but no middle. Others merely stop at page 384, having nothing more to say and leaving the reader frustrated, since there was no satisfactory conclusion.

Planning your novel is the first step. This does not necessarily require a detailed chapter by chapter summary, but it should outline the highlights of the plot and include a rough idea of the story line you are going to follow.

The Beginning. An effective beginning has three objectives: 1) suggest the conflict or problem that confronts the protagonist; 2) establish the setting; 3) introduce some of the main characters.

The Middle. This is the portion that adds to the course of the conflict, that starts the story on its way, through a series of increasing crises, toward the ultimate climax. The author must contrive to create and maintain suspense, while at the same time firmly establishing the role of the central character.

The Ending. Effective endings should be brief and satisfying, but also should have an element of surprise. While striving for the unexpected, the author should be certain that the conclusion is logical and believable. Avoid such contrivances as the use of coincidence or the sudden appearance of an identical twin in an effort to surprise the reader. Though coincidences occur in real life, they cause the novelist to lose his credibility.

Writing Short Stories

The short story has many of the same elements as a novel, except that it is compressed, with more emphasis on form, structure and plot than on characterization. A novel may have twenty or thirty characters, but a short story seldom has more than three or four, and of these usually only two are deeply involved in the conflict.

In the first few paragraphs, you must introduce the main

characters, set the scene clearly (where and when?), and specify the problem with which the characters are faced. Develop the situation and add complications for the hero until his or her predicament appears unsolvable. Finally, either through courage, brilliance or resourcefulness the protagonist solves the dilemma. The conclusion must be one based on the hero's own ingenuity, not by coincidence or a miracle from above.

Writing Nonfiction Books

Writing the nonfiction book requires, above all else, an enthusiasm for research. Whether you prefer to write biographies, history, how-to or travel books, you must find an excitement in searching the archives, interviewing and seeking new ideas. You must also have a talent for organizing your materials.

Once you have an idea that you are convinced is important, fresh, and of interest to the reading public, you should prepare an outline that is as complete as possible. You may discover, during your research, that the subject has already been overdone, and you may wish to discard it. Or you may decide that you have a new approach, a different slant that makes your treatment viable.

When attempting your first nonfiction book, your chances for success will be increased substantially if you select a subject about which you have some expertise. For example, should you be a do-it-yourselfer with quite a few projects to your credit, you might consider a book on "Don't Do It Yourself . . . Unless . . . ," or "Do It Yourself and Save a Fortune," etc.

Regardless of your choice, you will save yourself hours or weeks of research if you submit a proposal to several publishers before you get too involved in your project. Should your queries result in rejection, accept the disappointment and turn your creative energies in a different direction.

Should you have a desire to write biographies, select subjects who have led interesting or adventurous lives. This doesn't necessarily require that he or she be a famous person or a Hollywood celebrity (usually these have been overdone); your subject can be a little-known person who has contributed to his particular field, or who has done something spectacular, perhaps hiking along the Continental Divide from Canada to New Mexico, or following the trails of the pioneers from the Rockies to California.

Avoid writing your biography in chronological order. Start with an incident that will immediately grab the reader's attention and make him curious as to what will happen next. When writing biography, relate the subject to his environment, making him an integral part of the time and place in which he lived. Wallace Stegner, who is both historian and novelist, has written an outstanding biography titled, *The Uneasy Chair: A Biography of Bernard DeVoto*. As one of the reviewers said of the work, "It glides so effortlessly over formidable obstacles to treatment and interpretation that a sense of the achievement almost gets lost in the pleasure of reading. . . . It brings him [DeVoto] all back with a rush, the voice and presence and major figure in our lives he was . . ."

Closely related to the biographical genre is the writing of history. Today's historian must do more than research and relate the facts; his work must be as interesting and fascinating as a novel, filled with anecdotes and personal observations. I strongly recommend that the neophyte who finds this to be his field should read Rex Alan Smith's *The Carving of Mount Rushmore*, or his *Moon of the Popping Trees*, considered to be one of the best books on Indian history published in this century.

Another genre you might consider is travel books. For today's market, you must avoid the travelogue approach, in which you merely chronicle the places you have been. A successful travel book combines history with anecdotes and personalities. Don't write about areas that you haven't personally visited. You can obtain valuable information from travel brochures and reference material in encyclopedias and the library, but these should be used only as supplements to your personal knowledge and experiences as a visitor to these places.

Once you've resolved the question of the kind of writing you are qualified to do, and that you feel comfortable with, it is time to take your first step in actually becoming a writer— putting the words on paper. That is when the sweet agony begins.

Key Seven

A Time to Write

Of all literary forms, the novel has always been the most popular with the beginning writer, as well as the most difficult. The novel also utilizes most of the elements required in other writing areas, with the exception of poetry. For those reasons I'm going to use the novel as a prototype for this chapter. Whether fiction or nonfiction, the same principles of narrative, exposition, dialogue, and characterization apply. Even those components normally associated with fiction, such as suspense and crisis, are employed by many of today's nonfiction writers.

You have prepared yourself mentally, set your goals and defined your interests. You have learned the rudimentary rules of style and the basic ingredients of a successful literary creation. You are ready—almost—to write. The missing ingredient is the idea—the subject, the basic conflict, the plot. Today's novels must involve at least one of the following conflicts: Man against man; man against nature or man against himself. Robert Louis Stevenson contended that "The spice of life is battle; the friendliest relations are still a kind of contest; and if we would not forego all that is valuable in our lot, we must continually face some other person, eye to eye, and wrestle a fall whether in love or enmity. Every durable bond between human beings is founded in or heightened by some element of competition."

One of the most powerful novels to come out of World War II was Herman Wouk's *The Caine Mutiny,* an example of man vs. man—the saving of the ship and all lives on board by defying the captain and facing the death penalty for mutiny. James

Joyce's *Ulysses* is primarily man's struggle against himself; and Stevenson's *Robinson Crusoe* is based on man's struggle against nature.

Some authors, professing to be dedicated to the art of writing, maintain that 'real life' doesn't have plots, that these are fabricated devices, that the story must find its own path. Most of these writers will start a book, become bogged down, and never finish it. This attitude is the excuse used by those unwilling (or unable) to develop an adequate, logical plan or story line. The skilled novelist is not manipulating life or the way of the world, but is projecting its course.

What is a plot? It's a plan of literary composition, composed of a complication or causally related events. Aristotle understood plot as being the most important element of a literary work, "the end for which it exists."

Realism has become the by-word of most of today's fiction, telling it like it is. A forerunner of this movement was John Steinbeck in his classic, *The Grapes of Wrath*. But one should not accept this preoccupation with reality as a literal truth. The novelist must provide his readers with the illusion of reality—he must make the impossible sound possible. And, since real life is seldom a well-organized sequence of events, it is the function of the novelist to put them in order. He must build, scene by scene, the complications and the suspense. In the reader's mind there should be the question: Will the protagonist succeed in obtaining his objective?

As the story proceeds, the characters may reach a higher state of maturity, or be influenced by events; but they must remain unchanged as they move from crisis to crisis, until the climax and the denouement are reached. If, in order to resolve the complication the protagonist must act illogically or be inconsistent with his previous behavior, the author's credibility may be lost.

Closely related to plot is the theme of your novel. What is the purpose of your story? Most successful novelists today write to entertain the reader, but satisfying the reader is just as important, and this can happen only if your work has a meaning, a relationship to life. "Good triumphs over evil," for example, may be a trite theme, but it is still the one most widely used in popular fiction. The theme of Sinclair Lewis's *Main Street* is that the American town is stupid, vulgar, and ugly. Stephen Crane's *The Red Badge of Courage* tells the reader that "War is Hell." And Somerset Maugham's *Of Human Bondage* conveys the message of man's inhumanity to man. Samuel Butler's *The Way of All Flesh* concludes that a parent cannot live his child's life for him.

A common mistake made by the beginning writer is a tendency to preach to get the basic theme across to the reader. Your theme must be a natural outgrowth of the action and events.

Do not, in developing your idea, attempt to reach the stars. Begin with the assumption that you will not, at this stage, write the Great American Novel. Be content with a solid story, based on your personal knowledge and experience. Greatness usually arrives in many small steps.

Once you have decided on your idea, let it gel for a few days, mulling it over in your mind. As Ben Franklin wrote to a friend, "Before you sit down to write on any subject . . . spend some days in considering it, putting down at the same time, in short hints, every thought which occurs to you as proper to make a part of your intended piece."

After a period of meditation, prepare a synopsis. This will be your roadmap. Ask yourself if the plot and storyline are logical and believable, and if the theme is clearly defined.

Select your characters, then write about each of them in detail. Describe their physical characteristics, personalities, background, psychological traits and special quirks about the way they look, talk, or walk that will make them unique and memorable. Analyze the part they are going to play in your novel. Ask youself if you like the people you have chosen, if you find them interesting. Some of the greatest novelists start with a main character in conflict and build their entire storyline around him. Without strong characters who are identifiable and meaningful to the reader, your novel will lack the emotional appeal necessary to captivate your audience.

Madame Bovary is one of the best examples of a novel built around a character. As important as plot and scene may be in a work of fiction, your readers are more concerned with the characters than with the events. When you recall the great books you have read or the plays you have seen, it is the characters you recollect. Sherlock Holmes, Tom Sawyer, James Bond, Archie Bunker and Hamlet are remembered long after the plot has been forgotten.

"Generally the most vivid characters come out of the author's experience," writes Leon Surmelian in *Techniques of Fiction Writing*. "It is part of the writer's job to endow his characters with enough freedom to turn them loose.... Successful characters are people-in-tension, not always people-in-action." You must create flesh-and-blood characters with whom your readers can identify and even imagine themselves in the place of the hero or heroine. I think of this technique as the "Walter Mitty Syndrome."

Write down all of the vital statistics concerning your characters: when they were born, when they were married and the names and ages of their children. What about their occupations, hobbies and special interests? What kind of friends do they have, and what kind of enemies? Devote at least a full page of description to your main characters and keep it by your side.

Picture in your mind, much as an artist would before putting his brush to canvas, the time and place of each of your scenes. You may find arranging the scenes chapter-by-chapter works best for you. Be sure the events flow smoothly from one to the other, and that each is complete, preferably ending on a suspenseful note, with an impending urgency that will force the reader ever onward.

Many modern-day authors shun this approach, insisting that the art of story-telling requires that the characters determine the direction the novel will go. Even if you agree with this in principle, you should nonetheless have a plan in mind lest you discover yourself at a dead-end street before your story has been told. Julian Green, in *The Craft of Novel Writing*, points out that "should an author be too unmindful of the way in which his book is to be constructed, he might very well find himself in the plight of the Italian architect who hastily built himself a house and only when the roof was up, and each door in place, realized with a pang that he had forgotten the staircase."

As you get into the actual writing of your novel, you may

find that your characters have taken over, disregarding some of the signposts you included in your roadmap, but having your outline or synopsis will insure that you won't forget the staircase.

Once you have the characters, storyline and plot firmly in mind, select a specific time when you are going to start your first draft. At the appointed hour, let nothing interfere with your trip to the typewriter or word processor (or a pen and pad if that is more your style).

Write as rapidly as possible, with little attention to details. Don't clutter your mind with concerns as to grammar, spelling or the exact word. Let your unconscious mind have a free rein. As Dorothea Brande emphasizes in *Becoming a Writer*, "To be able to induce at will the activity of that higher imagination, that intuition, that artistic level of the unconscious—that is where the art's magic lies, and is his only true 'secret'."

Questions often asked of successful authors relate to their *modus operandi*. Clive Cussler, for example, begins with a prologue and continues through the chapters in sequence clear to the end. Faulkner preferred to use an anecdote or an expression. "I'll start from there and sometimes I write the thing backwards." He lets the characters dictate the course of action. "I'm dealing simply with people who suddenly have got up and have gotten into motion—men and women who are moving, who are involved in the universal dilemmas of the human heart."

The most popular approach is opening your novel with an event outside the character of the protagonist, but which starts a chain reaction of related incidents. You should immediately present a conflict or an impending crisis. Here's how Cussler's first sentence reads in *Cyclops*: "The *Cyclops* had less than one hour to live." Then, "In forty-eight minutes she would become a mass tomb for the 309 passengers and crew—a tragedy unforeseen and unheralded by ominous premonitions, mocked by an empty sea and a diamond-clear sky."

In *The Day the World Ended*, by Gordon Thomas and Max Morgan Witts, the reader senses the impending doom in the first seventy-five words: "There had been a rumbling from Mount Pelee for two weeks, deep-throated, muted, coming from the bowels of the earth. It had caused no panic in the town of St. Pierre, for the volcano had erupted only twice in three hundred years, and then only in scatterings of ash. Even in the third week in April, when the night sky was lit by flashes that resembled artillery fire, nobody was unduly concerned."

Nothing has actually happened, but the suspense has been created and the book is what editors call "a page turner." Is Mt. Pelee about to erupt? What will happen to the people in Saint Pierre if it does? The novel tells the melodramatic story of how this tragedy affected the people in this peaceful village. Again, as important to the story as the event was, the novel itself is about people—in this case man against nature.

Madame Bovary starts with Charles becoming a doctor, completely outside the main character, Emma, who had never even met Charles Bovary at the time. Nonetheless, this sets off a chain reaction of events to follow.

Tom Jones begins with Tom's birth as a supposed bastard, an event removed from the protagonist, but an incident which leads into related episodes.

An opening that magnetizes the reader not only impresses the editor who will decide the fate of your manuscript, but also stimulates you, the author, and creates the anxiety and urge you need to complete the work. Without this enthusiasm, you may become one of the silent majority of writers who never finishes that first novel, eventually filing it in a trunk piled high with unfulfilled dreams.

Not only should your schedule establish the days and time when you write, but also the number of hours you will spend at the typewriter. Teach yourself to start to work the minute you sit down at your machine. If you find yourself staring at a sheet of paper or a blank screen on your word processor, get up, take a brief walk around the house and then return to the task. Anthony Trollope, in his autobiography, states that he would sometimes write only a few pages a day, at other times as many as sixteen pages. "When my work has been quicker done—and it has sometimes been done very quickly—the rapidity has been achieved not by pressure, not in the conception, but in the telling of the story."

For purposes of practice, we are going to assume that you have developed your story idea and have your main characters firmly in mind. Now you will set a specific time when you are going to start Chapter One. It could be today, tomorrow, or next Wednesday.

As I've already indicated, some authors prefer to begin at the end, or in the middle, or no place in particular, but for this exercise you will start with the first chapter.

One decision you should make relates to the point of view—who is going to tell the story? It could be told from an omniscient viewpoint, with the author being able to read the minds of all of the characters; the more conventional method is the third person point of view, usually the protagonist; or it could be told in the first person, with the author as the storyteller. Some writers prefer to write the first draft in the first person to insure a consistent point of view, and then they subsequently change the viewpoint of the third person.

You've read examples of the introductory paragraphs of two novelists. What you should accomplish on the first page of your manuscript is the event that gets the action started (in *Cyclops* it was the sinking of the ship, and in *The Day the World Ended* it was the imminent eruption of Mount Pelee). Also on the first page should be a description of the scene, so that the reader will know where he is. Early in the first chapter introduce the protagonist or other main characters who will have a significant role to play in the outcome of your novel.

What else should you include in this opening chapter? In the classic, *Madame Bovary*, it was a major scene, a dramatic conflict between the school headmaster and Charles Bovary. Work into your big scene as soon as possible, and let it be the thread that weaves its way through your entire narrative.

In these early stages include a hint of what might follow, an inkling of a major disaster or a devastating conflict that will have a serious effect on your main characters. In the process you should develop a sympathetic concern for the protagonist, if he or she is the hero. Even if the protagonist is a villainous character, you should arouse an emotional response on the part of the reader. If your reader doesn't feel empathy for the characters, it won't matter how precarious a situation the hero may face; the reader will lose interest in the outcome.

Another essential in your first chapter is establishing the time and place, letting your readers know where they are. Imagine yourself as a playwright, setting the stage for the first act. The more realistic the scene, the more believable your story becomes, and the easier it is for your audience to become a part of the action.

One of the advantages a novelist enjoys is the ability to change scenes frequently, to create minor crises or diversions as well as to complement the major thrust of the novel's plot. This kind of variety serves several purposes: It is an excellent way to introduce lesser characters, to provide clues that may add to the suspense and to add complications to the story line.

In a novel, or any other form of writing, the beginning is the most important element. The second most essential component is the end of the first chapter. It must pose a question in the reader's mind: What is going to happen next? The movie makers of the early thirties were masters of this technique, especially those who were producing serials that continued for ten or twelve weeks. They recognized that the ending of an episode had to be gripping enough to bring the audience back a week later. Consequently, the final scene, without exception, would show the hero or heroine in an impossible situation— falling off a cliff, facing a ferocious lion or the young maiden tied to the railroad tracks with the train approaching at great speed.

Today's reader is too sophisticated to accept such melodramatic situations, but the premise hasn't changed. You must end the chapter dynamically, with an urgency that compels the reader to turn to that next page.

If you have successfully completed this exercise, you now have chapter one of your novel in rough draft form. Before finishing the assignment, write at least the first paragraph of the next chapter, stopping in the middle of a sentence, or the middle of your thought. Know where you are going before you quit. You'll find this will make the next day's work much easier.

For those who are interested in writing short stories, nonfiction articles or books, most of the same principles apply. Obviously the short story cannot have as many plot complications, nor as many characters. But the characters must be real to the reader, and the storyline must be plausible, with the ending, happy or sad, at least satisfying.

We've discussed characters, plot, theme and point of view as elements found in most novels. Two other essential ingredients are exposition and narrative. Exposition is the necessary window dressing that adds substance to your novel. It may be the description of a place, events, or characters, or a combination of these. The exposition should relate to the characters, and that the descriptions, like the action, be either personally observed or deduced from the characters. If the point of view is omniscient, it's possible that any of several characters could be the observers. If told from the third person point of view, only the narrator can be the observer.

Avoid the editorial approach, inserting yourself in the role of a travel director in your expository passages. Let the characters disclose the information, through dialogue, through reminiscences or through the use of a third person imparting his knowledge to the narrator.

The basic ingredient in any work of fiction is the narrative, simply defined as telling the story. What the novelist must do is condense the events, including only those that contribute to the plot. To expedite the movement of your story, combine your narrative with action. Try to make your narration dramatic, exciting. A good storyteller is one who keeps the reader on the edge of his chair, ever heightening the suspense from chapter to chapter.

Nonfiction articles or books must, like the novel, get off to a fast start, hook the reader immediately and offer a provocative or important problem which you promise to solve. Your article or book should include anecdotes and well-drawn characters, as well as a storyline with drama and suspense. Just as today's novelist must utilize many of the techniques required in nonfiction, such as comprehensive research to add reality, so the writer of nonfiction must borrow from the novelist the skills of dramatizing events and making the people he is writing about lively and interesting.

Regardless of the area of writing you have selected, the one essential that will determine success or failure is your ability to complete your project. Avoid the roadblocks, the alibis, the various excuses. Write rapidly, on schedule, until you have finished your first draft. Then it is time to take a few days off before the really hard work commences—polishing your work until it reflects the quality of your finest creative effort.

Key Eight

The Finishing Touch

After completing the first draft of your manuscript—the first of several—you should reward yourself by putting the project aside for a few days or a week before tackling the manuscript again.

If it's possible, take a vacation, a trip to the mountains or the seashore, or a Caribbean cruise. Or just enjoy your favorite sport or other leisure activity, whether it be fishing, golf, hiking in the woods or relaxing at the pool. Put the story out of your mind. Avoid the natural inclination to rehash it during this period.

When you feel ready to resume your work, read the entire manuscript, being as objective as possible, searching for major problems that must be solved. Does it flow logically? Does the plot come to a satisfactory conclusion? Do the characters appear to be alive? Does the story move at a good pace? Is it believable?

Your second draft should be more complete than the first, with most of the gaps filled in and grammatical and spelling errors corrected. While working on this phase, keep a thesaurus by your side, changing words to eliminate repetition or to make your style more colorful and your meaning more exact. This is the time to eradicate nondescript phrases which plague most authors. The novelist should employ his writing skills much like a painter uses his brush to achieve beauty, form, composition and interpretation.

The right word or expression in one circumstance may be entirely wrong in another. At times you may choose to generalize to avoid telling the reader too much. For example, when describing the weather, if unimportant to the progress of your story, you may say, "The weather had been lousy lately." If weather conditions play a role in your narrative, it is better to say, "The day before yesterday had been miserably cold with six inches of snow in the city. But yesterday the weather cleared and there wasn't a cloud in the sky." In describing a party, you might write, "It was a fun party," and let it go at that. If the event has significance to the plot, you need more details: "It was one of those affairs where the champagne sparkled, and we danced until dawn."

One question repeated at every workshop is, "How many times should I revise my story?" The answer is: As many times as necessary, or until you are convinced the manuscript is the very best you can produce. Some authors have the ability to write a single draft, making minor changes in subsequent revisions, while others may write as many as seven or eight versions.

If you have the discipline, put each draft aside for a few days, then come back to it, review the manuscript again, concentrating on the storyline, plot development and resolution. If your novel, for example, is one of mystery and intrigue, built around the plot, be certain there is a real conflict, a problem— a human problem that will involve the reader emotionally.

Is the central character faced with a conflict that forces him to take an action or make a difficult decision? The solution must be accomplished by the protagonist in a way that is logical and consistent with his past behavior. Here's a simple test you can apply to your plot: A person driven to do something; the doing becomes more difficult as the story progresses, followed by a satisfactory or conclusive end to the drive. If your story fails this test, you do not have a plot.

Many short stories, and occasionally novels, do not have a plot, merely presenting a situation or a problem. These are called 'slice of life' stories and are acceptable in today's marketplace. However, you still must have conflict and suspense, as well as dramatic episodes to maintain the reader's interest.

After analyzing the story's plot, take a close look at your characters. Probably the greatest single weakness in fiction is inadequate character development. Does the reader know what the hero and heroine look like? Do they have distinguishing features, meaningful gestures and mannerisms to help the reader identify them? Are they flesh-and-blood people, not merely stereotypes, who behave logically and consistently within the context of your story? To keep your readers emotionally involved in the drama they must believe in the reality of your characters and be concerned about their ultimate fate.

Every schoolboy remembers Ichabod Crane in Washington Irving's *The Legend of Sleepy Hollow.* And here's why: "He was tall, but exceedingly lank, with narrow shoulders, long arms and legs, hands that dangled a mile out of his sleeves, feet that might have served for shovels, and his whole frame most loosely hung together. His head was small, and flat at the top, with huge ears, large green glassy eyes, and a long snip nose, so that it looked like a weathercock perched upon his spindle neck to tell which way the wind blew. To see him striding along the profile of a hill on a windy day, with his clothes bagging and fluttering about him, one might have mistaken him for the genius of Famine, descending upon the earth or some scarecrow eloped from a cornfield." Ichabod, to every child who ever listened to the story, was a real person, someone children cared about.

What about the setting? Your story must not take place in a void. Whether it is science fiction, a gothic romance or a contemporary spy thriller, there must be points of reference, a time and a place. What months and years are covered by your story? Where does the action take place? Have you adequately described the setting, and are these descriptions woven into the story, not artificially included, as you might write descriptions in a travelog? Your depictions of the place must not be static, but should be a moving force contributing to the progress of your narrative in the same way that your character development and dialogue must bear upon the complications of the plot. One of the dangers is overdescribing, presenting too many unnecessary details. As a test, review one of your passages relating to a scene, asking yourself if every word you've included is essential to the story line.

Compare your descriptions of scenes with this paragraph from the short story, "Noon," by Joseph Conrad: "Before going down to his boat Babalatchi stopped for a while in the big open space where the thick-leaved trees put black patches of shadow which seemed to float on a flood of smooth, intense light that rolled up to the houses and down to the stockade and over the river, where it broke and sparkled in thousands of glittering wavelets, like a band woven of azure and gold edge with the brilliant green of the forests guarding both banks of the Pantai. In the perfect calm before the coming of the afternoon breeze the irregularly jagged line of tree-tops stood unchanging, as if traced by an unsteady hand on the clear blue of the hot sky. In the space sheltered by the high palisades there lingered the smell of decaying blossoms from the surrounding forest; a taint of drying fish, with now and then a whiff of acrid smoke from the cooking fires when it eddied down from under the leafy boughs and clung lazily about the burnt-up grass." Conrad's sentences are too long and complicated, but in his description he uses all of the important senses: sight, smell, and touch. His words convey vivid images, and the reader feels he is a part of setting.

The most difficult part of self-criticism, and the most important, is an analysis of your style. You may have the greatest idea for a story ever conceived; but unless it is well written, the chances are it will never see printer's ink.

Style is defined as the way you write, the words you use and how you put them together. To judge your style, select two or three paragraphs and analyze them microscopically. Have you used cliches or stock words that have lost their exact meaning, or are vague and meaningless—words such as 'nice,' 'pretty', 'viable', 'basic', 'lovely', 'really'? Have you used 'active' words that move the story along and conjure up images? Is every word necessary? One of the frequent complaints heard from editors is that the author's style is unimaginative, conventional, and dull.

During my days as an editor, I concluded that most beginning writers (and some of the more successful as well) overwrite, using four or five words when only one is required. Adjectives and adverbs are an essential part of writing, but they should be used sparingly. In dialogue, for example, the novice writes: "How are things going?" he asked, *smiling sweetly.* "Not too well," she replied *with a frown.* Avoid the obvious. Let the reader use his imagination instead of telling him more than he needs (or wants) to know.

Check the viewpoint used in your story. Preferable is a consistent third person point of view, with the protagonist as the narrator. One disadvantage is that the main character must be present at all times, or in some other way be made aware of the action. This is also true if the story is told in the first person. The omniscient point of view allows the author to enter the minds of the characters and provides more flexibility. Having selected the point of view you decide to use, you must be consistent throughout the narrative.

When writing nonfiction, many of the same principles apply. Your style, for example, should be lively and fresh, and the narrative fast-moving. The anecdotes should be original, clever, and meaningful. If you are writing about people, your characters should meet the same test as in the novel. They must be adequately described, logical and consistent, and come to life for the reader. Include unusual mannerisms or habits that set them apart from wax-like stereotypes.

As part of your personal criticism, ask yourself these questions: Is it interesting? Does it get off to a fast start? Is it educational, significant, or entertaining. Finally, if it had been written by someone else, would you enjoy reading it?

One of the more significant differences between fiction and non-fiction is the amount of research involved. Your nonfiction work probably will not be a completely new idea—someone has written about the subject before—and therefore your approach must be different and your manuscript must include new material. The more 'primary' source material you use, the more important—and acceptable to an editor—your work will be.

A primary source is the original source, such as the actual, hitherto unpublished, copy of a diary from a pioneer on the Oregon Trail. Personal interviews with experts or others who have first-hand knowledge of an event are also primary sources. A secondary source is material found in a published book, magazine, or newspaper.

Follow the same procedure with a nonfiction work as with a novel. Let it age for a few days. Then examine it closely, reading it objectively. And ask these questions: What about the opening?

Does it grab the reader? Does it entice him? Is it a "page-turner?"

Since readers identify more with people than events, build your book or article around characters. If possible without destroying its authenticity, dramatize your material and include realistic descriptions of action.

The use of dialogue not only makes the page of type less forbidding, but it also helps your material come to life. Your dialogue must be accurate. This does not mean that you must quote a person verbatim, including all the 'ahs' and 'you knows', but you should not fabricate a conversation merely to add excitement.

When reviewing your final draft, consider whether it would be enhanced by using photographs or other illustrations. More and more, editors are seeking articles and nonfiction books that are well illustrated. If you are writing history, seek out old photographs or drawings at your local historical society or library. For contemporary illustrations, you may decide to take up photography as a hobby that may easily pay for itself, or you can hire the services of a professional photographer. *Literary Market Place* not only lists photographers, but also artists and photographic agencies that have stock photos for sale.

For those who have chosen poetry as their literary objective, analysis becomes more difficult, since poetry by its very nature is a subjective form of writing.

Your questions should be: Is this a fresh, significant idea? Is it an original approach to the subject? Does the poem have a theme, an underlying meaning?

Check your poem for rhythm, beat and scanning. Does your poem have a regular beat or one that constantly varies? Count the number of syllables in your first line. Are the same number employed in each succeeding line? A wide variety of word or rhythm patterns may be used, but there must be consistency.

Even in free verse there must be a certain cadence. Read your poem aloud, emphasizing the beat. Do you stumble over some of the words? Are there unintentional rhymes or words that seem inappropriate? Attune your sense of hearing so you are sensitive to sound and to the flow of the words.

If rhyme is a part of your pattern, the poem does not have

to have end-line rhyme, but there should be consistency. Say the rhyming words aloud to be certain they rhyme. A poem needs variety in form just as much as it needs variety in word images. If every line ends with a comma or a period, the poem may become mechanical and boring. Enhance the appeal by running over two or three lines before coming to a complete stop.

Does your poem build to a climax, and, finally, has it accomplished the purpose you originally had in mind?

Poetry is one of the most difficult art forms, and one of the most gratifying for those who master the technique of writing it.

Having completed your revisions, and being convinced that your work is as perfect as you can make it, the time has come to write the final draft. Unless you are adept as a typist, employ a professional to do the final draft. One advantage, in addition to saving your time and obtaining a more attractive manuscript, is that a second set of eyes might see some errors you have overlooked. On the other hand, if you type the manuscript yourself, you might discover some areas that need improvement.

With the advent of the word processor, it makes sense to put your final draft on a disk for several reasons. If you find some minor errors on the print-out (or "hard copy," as it is called), they can be corrected easily, without retyping pages. Since most word processors have a "search and replace" feature, you can correct a character's name throughout the manuscript without physically reviewing every page. Also, there are software packages which will enable you to check the spelling and make corrections, and will give you an exact count of the total number of words in your manuscript.

You may have read that some editors will not accept manuscripts that are printed in 'dot matrix', since these are more difficult to read. However, most dot matrix printers today can also print in 'near letter quality', which is generally acceptable. The 'letter quality printers' produce the neatest finished product, but they are usually slower and more expensive.

The appearance of your manuscript provides editors with their initial impression of your work, so don't prejudice them against you before they even start to read your material. If you prefer a typewriter, use a fresh black ribbon. The paper should be a white, 20-pound bond, 8½ x 11″. Corrections should be clean and few, with no x'd out words or strikeovers.

A separate title page is not needed on any but book-length manuscripts. The first page in your manuscript should include your name, address, social security number and copyright notice in the upper lefthand corner; and the title and your byline (or pen name) in the center of the page about a third of the way down from the top.

Begin your first paragraph well below your by-line (quadruple space). Indent the first line of each paragraph five to seven spaces, but be consistent. Your entire manuscript should be double-spaced (not 1½ or 3), with no extra space between paragraphs.

If you want to set off a song or poem, a long quotation or excerpt from another work, etc., do so by indenting another two spaces. It is not necessary to put extra space between the excerpt and the main text, nor is it necessary to doublespace the body of the excerpt.

Leave a minimum of a one-inch margin on the left and a three-quarter inch margin on the right, and no less than a one-inch margin top and bottom. Type the same number of lines on each page (excluding page one and the first pages of chapters), and keep your character count as close as possible to the same for each line. This may seem overly fastidious, but it will simplify the editor's work should he decide to publish your manuscript. If you are using a word processor, these mechanical details are accomplished automatically. If not, you may wish to draw out a diagram for margins on a sheet of typing paper to be inserted between the original and the carbon.

Editors have different preferences as to the way running heads and page numbers should be placed. An acceptable practice is to place your last name, a brief title (or keyword), and page number in the upper right hand corner. For example: Bower/ Ten Keys/ -3-. Always number the pages consecutively, even in the case of a book with several chapters or sections.

A stamped, self-addressed envelope (SASE) should accompany each submission, except in the case of book manuscripts, in which case it is best to place the stamps unattached inside the box in which the manuscript is mailed. If your manuscript is less than four pages, it may be folded twice to fit a No. 10 envelope; between four and eight, it may be folded once. Any manuscript, regardless of length, can be sent flat, but if it has more than eight pages, it *must* be mailed flat. The return envelope should be slightly smaller so as to fit the outside cover without folding. When mailing a book-length manuscript place it in a heavy, corrugated mailer designed especially for the purpose.

A few don't's: Don't bind the manuscript in any kind of a cover. Don't staple or clip chapters or other parts together. Keep the pages loose. Don't attempt to enhance your manuscript by including your own concept of a cover design.

If you wish to enclose a cover letter, it should be brief and have something relevant to say. Should your material be technical, point out your credentials in your letter or in an attached resume.

Photographs or other graphics, if included, should be packaged separately and listed so they can be easily identified. Do not insert them between the pages of your manuscript, although you may wish to indicate on a sheet of paper that you plan to include a photograph or drawing in a particular place. Do not send irreplaceable originals, but make copies and explain to the editor that you have original prints or color transparencies available.

Any ruse you may use to determine if the editor has read your manuscript (such as turning pages upside down or gluing them together) will mark you as an amateur and irritate the editor.

On brief manuscripts or fillers, make a physical word count. For longer manuscripts, make an actual count of four or five pages, obtain an average and multiply by the total number of pages (unless your computer can do this for you). As a rough estimate, 250 words is the average per page if Pica type (large) is used, and 300 words if the type is Elite. Do not use an extra large or an extra small type, or any kind of exotic type face, such as script or Old English.

Word processors have the capability of italicizing words or

making them bold face. However, for the present at least, editors prefer that words you wish to italicize be underlined. The righthand margin can be justified with a word processor, but most editors prefer that the righthand margin be ragged (uneven).

If you feel there could be any doubt as to whether or not your manuscript has come to a close (!), you may use "End" or a triple # # #.

Some final precautions you should take before sending your manuscript to a publisher include (1) obtaining permission for any copyrighted material you may have used, and (2) checking your manuscript to be sure you have no libelous statements.

If you are sending your material to a publisher on speculation, you may wish to wait until you have a commitment before obtaining permissions for copyrighted material. But do not sign a contract until you have all of the permissions in writing from the copyright owner.

When writing for permissions, you should state the title and author of the book, the edition (first, second, etc.), the page numbers which include the material you are quoting, and the first and last part of the quotation. As a matter of courtesy, you should indicate that you will credit your source. In some cases, the copyright owner may request a fee, normally a nominal amount.

Under the 'fair use' doctrine of the present copyright law, you may use brief excerpts from copyrighted works without obtaining permission; but if in doubt, request the permission.

You are also responsible for any defamatory statements you may make about an identifiable person. In a nonfiction work, if you are quoting an individual, it may be wise to obtain a release. In a novel, should you use a real person as a model for any of your characters, disguise the individual as much as possible. Change his physical appearance, his line of work and the place where he lives. Using a disclaimer such as, "Any resemblance to any person is purely coincidental" is not an adequate defense in a libel suit.

At long last, your manuscript is ready to face the hard, cruel world of publishing. It is as carefully groomed as a royal prince at his wedding to the beautiful princess, as painstakingly constructed as a Frank Lloyd Wright architectural wonder, and as perfect in every detail as a Van Gogh masterpiece.

Once again, put it aside for a week. If you have an acquaintance who is qualified to criticize your work, you might ask him to read it.

Now you are ready to accept the challenge. The single cell you created on page one has developed into a complex and complete literary work. It is about to face the world.

Key Nine

Selling What You Write

Now is the time when you must march to the tune of a different drummer, and, having created a product, start devoting your energies to selling it. Successful authors write for the market—and unless you accept this premise your months of creative effort may end up as an exercise in futility.

Ideally, an author should query a number of publishing houses, outlining his idea briefly (but enthusiastically) before starting to write. (I discuss query letters in detail at the end of this chapter.) If his proposal results in rejection after rejection, without a word of encouragement along the way, he should face the reality that his idea may not be worth pursuing.

The contrary point of view is that one must persevere in the face of adversity. Jean and Veryl Rosenbaum make this observation in their book, *The Writer's Survival Guide:* "Since we must all expect rejections, it is imperative to develop sensible defenses against feeling annihilated by them.... We can approach rejections as a catalyst for improvement."

Editors are human beings and are subject to the frailties that exist in all of us, such as making errors in judgement. The number of books rejected by editors, only to eventually become best sellers, totals several thousand. What appeals to the editor at Harper & Row may be considered worthless trash by the editor at Simon & Schuster.

At an American Booksellers Convention luncheon, I was seated next to the editor of a major publishing house who told me that he had rejected *Jonathan Livingston Seagull*, and even after it had become a bestseller he said he would reject it again. Cass Canfield, senior editor at Harper and Row, recalls that *The Peter Principle* was turned down by 16 or 17 houses. One of the editors at Harcourt, Brace, Jovanovich (who shall remain nameless) turned down Mac Hyman's *No Time for Sergeants*, *Lolita*, Norman Mailer's *Deer Park*, and *The Godfather*. As an experiment, two frustrated writers retyped the first two chapters of *War and Peace*, changed the title and submitted it to a dozen different publishers. They received four form rejections, three letters from editors advising that "it doesn't meet our requirements," and only two recognized it for what it was. The conclusion is that the writer must try, and try, and try again, hoping he will eventually reach the right editor at the right time.

Significant changes in the marketplace have occurred over the past twenty years, both in magazine and book publishing. Magazines are divided into many more groups today, such as religious, confessions, business, hobbies, men's, women's, travel and sports, and within these, additional specialization has taken place. Virtually every magazine has a very rigid policy which determines the kind of material it uses. Editorial requirements have become tailored to give each magazine its own individual characteristics. However much one may learn from market tips, there is no substitute for reading the magazine and studying it.

Some markets are wide open for the freelancer, others use freelancers occasionally, and some are completely closed, employing staff writers for all of their material. Unfortunately, more magazines are shutting the door on freelancers, partially due to budget cuts and partially to a lack of quality manuscripts being submitted by freelancers.

A few decades ago the short fiction market was burgeoning, and many of the greats started their careers writing for the pulps. Although the pulps have disappeared, more of the popular general magazines, such as *Redbook, Esquire, McCalls, Playboy* and *Saturday Evening Post*, have been increasing their use of fiction in recent years. These markets, however, are extremely competitive, and offer limited opportunities for the beginning writer.

But there are numerous fiction markets available to those authors who have not achieved a reputation. Prolific users of fiction are the juvenile, religious, science fiction, fantasy, confessions, and the literary or 'little' magazines often sponsored by educational institutions. For the most part, these depend largely upon unsolicited freelance submissions. Payment is generally low (often in copies of the magazine), although their demand is for high quality material.

Many of the juvenile magazines are religious in concept, and consequently it is necessary to understand the religious principles advocated by such publications. A growing market exists for adult religious or inspirational material, but again the writer must be aware of the particular tenets to which the publication adheres.

Almost all of the confession magazines (which are largely fiction, contrary to such titles as *True Story* and *True Confessions)* depend entirely on freelance submissions. Once a writer establishes credits in this market, it can be a steady source of income. These magazines have become more sophisticated in recent years, requiring a strong theme and stories based on actual experiences.

Another expanding market for fiction has been created by an influx of new women's magazines which have evolved as a result of the female liberation movements. Since many of these appear and disappear suddenly, the writer should check the latest market guides for changes.

Except for the sexually oriented magazines, the best possibilities for men's fiction exist in the areas of science fiction, fantasy, and mystery. A market largely overlooked is the semifictional men's magazines, such as *Amazing Detective, True Police Cases, True Detective*, etc., which use material based on actual police cases with some fictionalizing. Timeliness is important here, since these magazines depend for their success on being the first to report a crime case. A generation ago, they would publish accounts before the suspect went to trial; but with the present interpretation of the laws, all crime stories now are published after a guilty verdict has been rendered. To make it in this field, you should become well acquainted with the law enforcement agencies in your area and establish rapport with newspaper photographers, since photos are essential.

Many more opportunities are available if you are writing nonfiction articles. So extensive is this market that almost any kind can be sold if written in an interesting manner and avoiding trite, overworked subjects. Outlets for nonfiction are even more specialized than for fiction, so knowledgeable marketing is absolutely essential. The types of markets loosely fall into the seven different categories listed below. The main requirement is that your material comes from authoritative sources, is derived from personal experiences, or is obtained through extensive research and interviews.

The General Market. The slicks, women's magazines, men's magazines, and other consumer magazines usually devote a maximum amount of space to articles. Most of these are written by highly experienced writers, frequently on assignment. Some magazines will buy ideas for articles, which are then assigned to staff writers. But the beginning freelancer can sell to this market if his work is comparable in style, execution, and comprehensiveness to that of established writers.

The Opinion Magazines. Magazines like *U.S. News & World Report, Time, New Republic,* and *The Nation* offer a market only to those who are able to draw on their own meaningful experiences or skillful interviews with authorities or political figures. The university quarterlies, such as *Yale Review, Chicago Review, Kenyon Review, Southwest Review,* as well as national monthlies (*Atlantic* and *Harper's,* for example) use thoughtful and significant articles, but again it is the exceptional writer, equipped with both writing talent and sound information, who will gain acceptance in these publications.

The Specialized Markets. These publications run the gamut from sports and outdoors to animal magazines. Also in this category are movie, Western, history, military, regional, city, and travel magazines. Many use a considerable amount of freelance material, much of it based on personal experience, unusual events or interviews with well-known or interesting personalities.

The Technical Magazines. These periodicals, covering business, music, garden and home, health, science, economics, automotive and aviation, are quite receptive to freelancers who know their market. In recent years there have been a rash of magazines related to the computer industry, but many of these are short-lived, so once again it is important to check the latest market information to be certain the publication still exists.

The Inspirational or Religious Magazines. This is an excellent market, with more than 90 percent of the editorial content written by freelancers. Virtually any subject will be considered, provided it is carefully researched, based on personal experience, and has a definite upbeat conclusion. Preaching or over-moralizing are taboos. The juvenile publications in this field have become much more liberal in their editorial views and are breaking away from strict parochial limitations. Many deal with current problems, such as racism, drugs, permissiveness, family harmony, etc. This is also an excellent market for short material and fillers: inspirational essays, short humor, jokes, puzzles, Bible quizzes and games.

The Trade Magazines and House Organs. Largely overlooked by the beginning writer is the trade journal and house organ market, which offers the best opportunity for the freelancer who wishes to make a steady income. Thousands of these publications exist, and editors are constantly on the lookout for qualified writers and are eager to work with those freelancers on whom they can depend. You must be willing to go out into the field to study an industry and to interview key personnel. Since most of the articles used include photographs, you should either learn the art of photography yourself or arrange to have a professional photographer work with you. Payment varies widely, from $50.00 to $800 or more, but once you have established yourself with a few of these magazines, you'll start getting regular assignments.

The Sunday Supplements. Many of the large daily newspapers publish magazine supplements (unfortunately the number is diminishing) using fiction, articles, and poetry. The material must have a local or regional slant, and payment is rather low. The *Editor and Publisher Yearbook* lists all of the newspapers in the U.S., and indicates which publish Sunday supplements. The national supplements, such as *Parade*, have a much broader appeal, but frequently use their own staff writers and seldom accept material from a freelancer unless the subject is exceptional, such as an exclusive interview with a celebrity or some unusual event witnessed first-hand by the writer.

The Poetry Market. Every conceiveable form of poetry may be salable, or at least acceptable to some publication. Literary magazines often cater to the far-out, experimental and off-beat poet. Others prefer sentimental poems written in rigidly conformist style. The 'little' magazines, usually sponsored by colleges or universities, represent a prolific market, though payment is more often than not in copies of the magazine. A word of caution about the vanity poetry publishers, who will accept any poem, good or bad, if the author agrees to purchase a copy of the anthology in which it appears.

Many newspapers, including small weeklies, occasionally will print poems, especially if they have a strong local interest. A few dailies have a poetry column and pay a rather nominal fee (seldom more than $25.00).

The best-paying and most prestigious magazines that use a limited amount of poetry are *Atlantic* and *Harper's*, but these publications generally do not accept poetry from unknowns.

A few of the larger publishers issue occasional volumes of poetry, providing the author has accumulated some credits in reputable poetry magazines (not vanity anthologies). The best opportunity for the lesser-known poet who wishes to publish a volume of his work is to seek out the smaller presses or self-publish.

Televison and Movie Markets. Shortly after the advent of television, books and courses flourished proclaiming this new medium as a bonanza for writers. Unfortunately, this horn of plenty proved to be as elusive as riches from the Pikes' Peak Gold Rush—few made the promised fortunes, and thousands ended their quest in despair and failure. Chances of the freelance writer selling a script to a television producer are remote. Legitimate studios will consider material only if it comes to them through a recognized agent or from an active member of the Screenwriter's Guild, and even then, the chances of making a one-shot sale are less than hitting the jackpot in Las Vegas.

Success in television is reserved for those who have an established reputation, either as a screenwriter or a best-selling novelist, unless, of course, you have a good friend in the business. As in most other areas of writing, the scriptwriter must start at the bottom. To repeat the suggestion made in an earlier chapter, contact little theatres in your community that produce dramatic scripts and often use local talent. Your cable television company might also consider using your material.

Movie producers, like their competitors in TV, will not normally consider or even read an unsolicited manuscript. Only if the material is submitted through a recognized agent will it be given any consideration. However, studios frequently purchase rights to novels, stage plays, or magazine fiction. Your chances for acceptance are far better if you have written a successful book or have had a play produced for the New York stage. Seldom does a playwright start his career with a Broadway production; more often he begins by writing for summer theatres, local theatrical groups, or the educational theatre.

The Book Publishing Market. Dramatic changes have occurred in the field of book publishing in the past decade, with many consolidations and purchases of book publishing companies by large corporations in unrelated fields. Family-owned houses, such as Alfred A. Knopf, Simon & Schuster, Dodd Mead, McGraw Hill and Harper & Row have been absorbed by conglomerates, and only the family name remains.

With these changes has come a greater emphasis on profits and an insistence by management that there be less risk-taking. Add to this, skyrocketing production costs, and a situation results that makes it more difficult for the unknown writer to get his first book accepted by a major publisher.

On the optimistic side is the rise in the number of paperbacks being produced, opening up dozens of new markets for the beginning writer. Most paperbacks (or soft cover) some years ago were reprints of hardcover titles that had been successful. Today, the majority of paperbacks are originals, and frequently a book will be published first in paperback and later in hardcover.

Book writing is the most challenging and can be the most rewarding, and at the same time the most frustrating area of literary endeavor. Some of the statisticians in the publishing field have estimated that 500,000 novels are started each year, and of these 100,000 may be completed eventually, with less than one percent of first novels ever being published. Considering that the sale of most first novels averages about 4,000 copies with royalties to the author of $5,000 or $6,000, and since most full-length books usually require at least two years of work, the financial rewards are less than the minimum wage.

As depressing as it may appear, book editors are hungry for new writers, and hope that in the stack of unsolicited manuscripts on their desks one might be a precious gem written by a housewife pecking away at her typewriter at the kitchen table, or a Western ranch hand banging out his manuscript on a tired old Underwood. Somewhere there might be another Steinbeck or Hemingway, another Louis L'Amour or Janet Dailey. It is a euphemism in the publishing world that even the greatest authors were at one time unpublished writers.

You can improve your chances for acceptance by choosing a genre that is in vogue at a particular time. For example, in the fifties and sixties, the gothic romance ranked high in paperback sales. As this form died out, it was replaced by the contemporary romance novel. The Western enjoyed great popularity until twenty years ago; then it fell into disfavor but eventually regained the spotlight. Mysteries and spy novels seem to hold their own over the years, and science fiction continues to maintain a good share of the market, although changed in concept, becoming far more sophisticated than in earlier times. Historical fiction, spurred in some degree by the success of James Michener's works, will usually get a favorable reading by today's book editors.

For the nonfiction author, the same criteria for determining the best markets apply. How-to and self-help books outnumber most other types of nonfiction, with over 2,000 titles currently in print. Self-help books dealing with health, exercise, beauty care, money management, investment strategies and personality improvement are always in demand.

In interviews with several book publishers, I was told that biography and history are editorial priorities for the Atlantic Monthly Press, Charles Scribners' Sons, Dell Publishing, and George Brazilier, Inc., as well as many others. An area increasing in popularity is the inspirational field, with more of the larger publishers entering that arena.

I also asked these editors why most of the unsolicited manuscripts are rejected, and here are some of their answers:

"Too similar to books already in the marketplace."

"An insufficient market for the material offered."

"Poor writing. Lackluster thinking, lack of potential salability."

"Do not fit our market. Also, non-writers who think they can write."

"Manuscript deals with subject matter that has been flooded, or is a dead subject area."

The Juvenile and Young Adult Market. This market is divided into various age brackets, and it is important for the writer to make sure his material is designed for a particular group. The illustrated children's book generally should be slanted to those who are 3 to 8. For the younger ages, it should be a "Read to Me" format. If slanted to the 5 to 12 age group, writers should use the vocabulary that is both understandable and readable by the child. From 12 to 18, considered the young adult novel, the reader is much more sophisticated today than he was ten or 20 years ago, and the plot, theme, and style should resemble that of an adult book.

Books for younger children, according to the editors I surveyed, should be animal stories or simple adventures. But trends for the young adult are toward mysteries, thrillers, famous characters, and science, with a growing market for contemporary romances slanted toward the teen-age girl.

Some reasons for rejection: lack of originality; dull, pedestrian writing; unimportant idea; not written at the proper level. Unless you have a sincere interest in children and a talent for understanding them, prepare yourself for rejections.

If you are writing an illustrated children's book, do not attempt to do the drawings yourself. Many publishers prefer to use their own artists, but should they ask you to furnish illustrations, seek out a competent professional and arrange to divide the royalties or pay him or her an outright fee. Don't, however, commit yourself until you have a contract from a publisher.

Finding the Right Market. As I've mentioned earlier, one of the best ways to determine what magazine or book publisher might be interested in your work is to study the various magazines, read the book lists put out by publishers, browse in your local bookstores, and read the advertisements and Forthcoming Books section of *Publishers Weekly.*

In addition to following these procedures, refer to current issues of the writers' magazines listing the editorial needs of various publications. Some of the national writers' organizations also publish newsletters including market information, usually for a specific area (such as travel, science fiction, romance, etc.). One of the more general newsletters is called *Market Update,* published as a section in the National Writers Club magazine, *Authorship. The Writer* includes a listing of different types of markets in each issue (one issue is devoted to book publishers, another to short stories, etc.). *Writer's Digest* devotes a column in each issue based on interviews with New York editors concerning their requirements.

There are numerous market directories available, most of them published on an annual basis. Some of the better ones are:

Literary Market Place (LMP). This is probably the best source for book publishers. It provides names of all the key personnel and their areas of responsibility, which enables you to write to a specific editor. It includes a minimum of information, however, concerning editorial requirements. Published by R.R. Bowker Company.

Writer's Market. This includes the most comprehensive general listing of popular markets and is especially valuable for its magazine listings and information concerning editorial requirements, rates of payment, how to submit material, plus brief articles on writing. Published by Writer's Digest.

Writer's Handbook. This is not as comprehensive as the *Writer's Market,* but includes excellent listings of TV and play markets. The breakdown of magazine markets into 'fiction', 'article', and 'popular' is helpful. Approximately two-thirds of the book is devoted to significant articles on writing technique. Published by The Writer.

Standard Periodical Directory. This directory has over 60,000 listings of periodicals of all kinds, including house organs and trade journals, but provides only a minimum of information concerning editorial requirements. Published by Oxbridge Publishing Company.

Standard Rate and Data (SRDS). This series of publications is designed primarily for advertising agencies. It publishes directories monthly covering consumer magazines, farm publications, business publications, newspapers and television, with a minimum of editorial requirement information. The primary advantage to the writer is that these directories are updated monthly and provide the best source for new publications. Only periodicals accepting advertising are included. Published by Standard Rate and Data Service.

Ayer Directory of Newspapers and Periodicals. This is one of the most complete listings available of daily and weekly newspapers (including Sunday Supplements), foreign language newspapers, trade publications and feature syndicates. It also lists general circulation magazines. No information on editorial requirements is included. Published by N.W. Ayer & Son.

Editor and Publisher Yearbook. This is the best source for names and addresses of U.S. and foreign newspapers, and for listings of syndicates and press services. Published by Editor and Publisher Company.

The Writers and Artists Year Book. This is the best source for writers looking for foreign (English language) publishers. Its major emphasis is on British and Irish markets, as well as journals and magazines in Australia, New Zealand and Africa. Theatre, film, radio and television markets also listed. Also some excellent articles about writing. Distributed in the U.S. by Writer's Digest Books.

International Directory of Little Magazines and Small Presses. This is the most comprehensive listing available of small publishers and little-known magazines, markets offering the best opportunity for the beginning writer and for avant-garde or off-beat material.

National Trade & Professional Associations of the U.S. and Canada. Technically this is not a market directory for writers, but a comprehensive listing of most of the associations in the United States and Canada, many of which publish newsletters, research reports or magazines for their members.

Having decided which are the most promising markets for your material, you should write a query letter if you are proposing a book-length manuscript or an article requiring considerable research. It is not necessary to query an editor concerning a short story or poetry.

Three basic principles that apply to query letters are: 1) keep it brief, 2) keep it informal and lively, 3) give the editor the information he needs to make an intelligent decision about your material—in such an enticing way that he will choose to see more.

During my years as an editor, I talked to numerous authors who insisted that the only way a fair appraisal of their work could be made was for me to read it in its entirety. If a writer cannot compose a convincing query letter, his or her book probably lacks organization or a clear-cut theme. A query letter's main purpose is to convince the editor that your idea is intriguing, important, and of vital interest to his readers.

A query letter to a book publisher or a magazine editor requires the same pre-preparation and the same calculated effort to 'sell' the editor. While it is unethical to submit complete manuscripts to more than one publisher at a time, there is no limit as to the number of queries you can send simultaneously. Each query should be individually typed and addressed to a specific editor. It is not a good policy to admit that you're sending out multiple queries, until you have a well-established reputation, sufficient to make it feasible to auction your work.

Your proposal should include specific information: The approximate number of words that will be in your finished manuscript; whether there will be illustrations, and if so, what kind and how many; when you anticipate completing the manuscript. If relevant to the project, include your credentials, stating why you are qualified to write the book.

Your opening statement must arouse the editor's interest. One editor of a major publishing house told me, "We want the author to seduce us with his or her idea."

Quickly give the editor the substance of your article or book and why it should have appeal to his readers. A brief quotation from the work itself, or an anecdote, may give the editor the flavor of the piece as well as an indication of how your writing sparkles.

Instead of asking the editor if you may send your manuscript, say that you will be pleased to send completed chapters, a detailed outline, or the finished manuscript if this is what the editor wishes.

The following is a query letter which resulted in the authors obtaining a book contract and a substantial advance from a major publisher.

Dear Mr. (Editor's Name and Title):

The world of singles is rapidly developing its own special kind of population explosion, resulting in its own kind of problems, lifestyle and solutions.

Until now, the emphasis has primarily been on the man or woman in his/her twenties or thirties . . . ignoring current statistics which show that today we have a higher percentage of single people over the age of 50 than ever before recorded!

Would you be interested in a nonfiction book about these more mature divorcees, widows, bachelors and bachelorettes?

For 18 months we have been involved in an in-depth study, having intimate interviews with hundreds of single people over 50, who are living successful, productive, self-fulfilled lives. The book we propose reveals their secrets and provides a sensible, logical and exciting way for others in their 50's, 60's, 70's, yes, even in their 80's, to find happiness, satisfaction, contentment—even thrills!

'I feel as if I've gotten off the battlefield,' one 57-year-old woman confided in us at a Realities of Divorce seminar we conducted at the University of Colorado.

One silver-haired male executive, a widower for nine years, said, 'I didn't think I could survive when my wife died. But I enjoy my time alone—not loneliness.'

'Until now,' a 65-year-old woman stated, 'no one has asked me how *I feel* about being single at my age, in this world that is so different from when I grew up.' She is typical of the hundreds who shared with us how they dealt with, and overcame, shock of loss, abandonment, despair, guilt and anxiety, stress and tension, how they developed new friendships, how they handle the new sex scene, and how they turned hidden talents into profit. They openly explain how they adjust to grown children living at home, managing money, getting or keeping jobs, and special situations of health, eating and energy.

What they have shared with such candor, sensitivity and honesty was virtually unexplored until now. This book is more than a how-to book. It provides both wit and wisdom for the reader, as well as an inspiring and imaginative way to pursue a new life.

This book will provide positive evidence that a single man or woman over 50 is not 'over the hill', but is rather on the crest of the most enriching and rewarding period of life. These people are having a wonderful time. Their observations have meaning.

We would like to show you a proposal and sample chapter of this exciting project.

(Signed by the authors)

P.S. Our credentials for doing such a book are enclosed.

The book, entitled, *Single After Fifty: How to Have the Time of Your Life*, by Beverly Anderson and Adeline McConnell, was published by McGraw-Hill.

Keep accurate records as to where and when you submitted your query letters and your manuscripts, plus any special notations editors may have made if your material is returned. Allow a reasonable time for the editor to reply. Publishers generally will answer a query letter within 4 or 5 weeks, but a book manuscript may be held for four or five months.

I'm sure many of you are asking the question: "Wouldn't it be better to get a literary agent who could do all of this marketing for me?" Unless you already have published one or more books, or have a book contract, few legitimate agents are going to be interested in accepting you as a client. Notice the word 'legitimate'. Agents who advertise for clients usually earn their income from charging substantial reading and editorial fees, not from commissions received from an author's royalties. Contrary to the neophyte's belief that the primary function of an agent is to 'sell your book', the truth is that an agent is most helpful in obtaining the best terms, handling subsidiary rights, or at times assisting in the promotion of your work, such as arranging appearances on talk shows or setting up autograph parties.

It is better for the beginning writer to handle all of the details of marketing himself, obtaining acceptance from a publisher before exerting time-consuming effort in usually fruitless attempts to secure a literary agent.

Once you have submitted your manuscript, occupy yourself with other projects. Try to keep a number of manuscripts in the mail at all times; and if one of your novels or articles is returned, immediately send the material to another publisher.

Don't allow yourself to become discouraged. As Loula Grace Erdman advised in *A Time to Write*, "Perhaps it is good for a writer to experience frustration and heartache and despair and yes, even rejection. It gives sympathy and understanding and compassion not only to one's writing, but to all the other experiences of life. In writing, as well as in living, we need to have a restraining hand laid upon us occasionally. It is entirely possible that we learn more from our failures than from our successes. . . . As the lyric says, 'Without hurt, the heart is hollow.' And when did anything good ever come from a hollow heart?"

The opposite of failure is success. And the next and final key will tell you how to deal with success.

Key Ten

How to Accept Success

You've met all the challenges, followed the rules and have revised and polished your creation and are convinced that it is the very best you can do. Your manuscript has been mailed and its fate (and yours) is now in the hands of the editor you so carefully selected.

Suddenly the mailman becomes a VIP, and you anxiously await his arrival each day. You become impatient after the first few weeks, but resist the temptation to inquire about the status of your material, fearful that this move might upset the editor and prejudice him against you.

What seems an eternity finally passes, and you receive a reply, along with your manuscript. "We are sorry," says the printed slip, "but this does not meet our editorial requirements. This is no reflection on the quality of your work." You recall the advice you have heard about persistence, and after a brief period of depression you submit it again, and again, and again.

Then, one day you find in your mailbox a letter, not the large brown self-addressed envelope you had submitted with your manuscript, but a personal letter from the editor advising you that he likes your manuscript and has enclosed a contract for you to sign. He might also express some reservations and suggest, in a general way, changes that should be made.

If this is your first book contract, your inclination is to sign it immediately before the editor changes his mind. At this point you are convinced that you have finally arrived and it will be just a matter of time until the royalty checks start arriving and you become a national celebrity.

But now is the time to be wary, to end the state of euphoria you are in, and turn into a business person. Put aside the adoration you may feel toward this publisher who wants your book and become aware of the fact that, although he may be willing to publish your book, his primary objective is to obtain it on the best possible terms. You become his adversary. Assuming that the contract you receive is 'our standard contract' is the first mistake most beginning authors make. More realistically, the agreement you are asked to sign is one designed to favor the publisher, and is subject to change.

Should you have a competent literary agent, it is his responsibility to review the contract and make changes that will be to your benefit. Agents have not been discussed, since those who are reliable and have a reputation among publishers generally will not accept unpublished writers. As mentioned in Key Nine, once you have a contract you might consider obtaining an agent to represent your interests.

The writer who has not had a book published is in a weak bargaining position, and is also fearful of suggesting changes that might cause the publisher to change his mind about publishing the book. Usually such fears are unfounded, since once the publisher has made a commitment, he is unlikely to reverse his decision.

There are major danger areas in most book contracts that the author should be aware of, and some changes that he should insist upon, even at the risk of losing the contract. Here are a few points of special importance to you as the author:

Royalties. Normally the author is offered a ten percent royalty on a hardcover book, with a sliding scale to 15 percent as the number of books sold increases. A word of caution: Some contracts will state that the royalty is based on 'net receipts' rather than on the 'retail price.' Since most books are sold to wholesalers at a 50 percent discount, the net receipts are only half of the retail price and therefore the author's royalty, likewise, is actually five percent instead of ten percent. Most publishers offer five or six percent of the retail price on paperback books, but usually a minimum of 25,000 copies are printed (as compared to 4,000 for a hardcover), resulting in more real income for the author.

Advances. It is accepted practice among legitimate publishers to offer an advance against royalties, with half of this advance paid upon signing of the contract, and half at the time of publication. In some instances one-third will be paid upon signing, one-third upon delivery of the manuscript, and one-third upon publication. Since this is an advance against royalties, the amount will be deducted from your royalty statements. It is important for you to receive an advance as a show of good faith on the part of the publisher, and to add validity to the contract. If the publisher has no monetary investment, he may decide at some later date to postpone publication for an indefinite period. Established writers may obtain a $25,000 advance or more, but the first-time novelist may have to settle for as little as $1,000.

Publication Date. You should insist that the contract include a proposed publication date, normally between 12 and 24 months from the time a final manuscript is submitted. If no publication date is indicated, the contract has no meaning for the author, since the publisher could tie up a particular manuscript for an indefinite period of time if he wished, especially if he did not pay an advance.

Option Clause. The best option clause in a contract is no option clause. The worst option clause is one stating that the publisher has an option on your next work, and *on the same terms as the present contract.* Should your first book be a best-seller, you normally would be in a position to bargain for better terms on your next book, *unless your first contract included the phrase, "on the same terms as the present contract."*

Copyright. Under the provisions of the Copyright Law which became effective January 1, 1978, an author owns the copyright to his manuscript from the time of its creation. The contract, therefore, should state that the book will be copyrighted in the author's name.

These are the main considerations, but you should also be aware of the terms offered in the contract for subsidiary rights, such as book club rights and foreign, movie, dramatic, and TV rights. An agent or an attorney knowledgeable in literary matters can be of help in determining what your fair share should be.

Contracts for shorter works, such as articles or short fiction, may or may not be required by a magazine publisher. If you should be asked to sign an agreement with a magazine, a serious danger exists if a statement is included that says "the work is being done for hire." At the present time, should you sign such an agreement, you give up *all rights* to your material. The publisher is not required to give you a by-line or any credit for the material, and any income he receives from reprints or other sources belongs to him. Attempts are being made by several writers' organizations to have this provision of the copyright law eliminated or revised.

Once you have signed your book contract and submitted your final manuscript to the publisher, you will be assigned an editor (normally it will not be the editor with whom you originally corresponded) to work with you, suggesting revisions, and copy-editing your manuscript. Some editors will make extensive changes, while others will change your manuscript very little. Feel free to disagree with any revisions that are made, and insist that you have the right to approve any changes that are made.

As far as the overall book design, the jacket or other production details, the author has virtually no control. Even the title decision ultimately is the prerogative of the publisher, although you have an opportunity to debate the issue.

Before your manuscript goes into production and is sent to the typesetter, you will be asked to give your final approval. Be sure you have made all the changes you wish to make at this point, since your contract will state that changes you make in the galley proofs (author's changes) will be at your expense if they exceed ten percent of the composition costs.

A word about reading proofs: It will save time and avoid possible mistakes if you are familiar with the accepted style of the publisher and with proofreader's marks. Since most publishers use the *Chicago Manual of Style* as a guide, you should refer to this, both for style and proofreading symbols.

After you have returned the galleys, you will shortly thereafter receive page proofs and also a proof of the cover design. Should your book require an index, you will be able to accomplish this

PROOFREADER'S MARKS

⊙ Insert period

⁀ Insert comma

:/ Insert colon

;/ Insert semicolon

? Insert question mark

⩔ Insert apostrophe

⩔⩔ Insert quotation marks

/=/ Insert hyphen

—|M Insert em dash

—|N Insert en dash

Insert space

✓✓✓ Equalize space between words(in text)

eq.# Equalize space between words(in margin)

∧ Caret--to mark exact position of error

⊗ Broken letter

𝒹 Delete

⊂ Close up

𝒶 Delete and close up

ls Letterspace

Begin new paragraph

No # No paragraph

‖ Align vertically

= Align horizontally

⊐ Move right

⊏ Move left

⊓ Move up

⊔ Move down

⊐⊏ Center

∩ Transpose(in text)

tr. Transpose(in margin)

sp. Spell out

--- Let it stand(text)

stet Let it stand(margin)

lc Lowercase(in margin)

≡ Uppercase(in text)

Cap Uppercase(in margin)

C+sc Set in small capitals

——— Set in italic(in text)

ital. Set in italic(margin)

∿∿ Set in boldface(text)

bf. Set in boldface(margin)

w.f. Wrong font

/ Used in text to show deletion or substitution

It does not appear that the earliest printers had any method of correcting errors before the form was on the press. The learned The Learned correctors of the first two centuries of printing were not proofreaders in our sense. They were rather what we should term office editors. Their labors were chiefly to see that the proof corresponded to the copy, but that the printed page was correct in its latinity--that the words were there, and that the sense was right. They cared but little about orthography, bad letters, or purely printers errors, and when the text seemed to them wrong they consulted fresh authorities or altered it on their own responsibility. Good proofs, in the modern sense, were impossible until professional readers were employed, men who had first a printer's education, and and then spent many years in the correction of proof. The orthography of

English, which for the past century has undergone little change, was very fluctuating until after the publication of Johnson's Dictionary, and capitals, which have been used with considerable regularity for the past 80 years, were previously used on the miss or hit plan. The approach to regularity, so far as we have, may be attributed to the growth of a class of professional proofreaders, and it is to them that we owe the correctness of modern printing. More errors have been found in the Bible than in any other one work. For many generations it was frequently the case that Bibles were brought out stealthily, from fear of mental interfence. They were frequently printed from imperfect texts, and were often modified to meet the views of those who published them.

task after receiving the page proofs. If you don't have the time or the talent to index the book yourself, your options are to hire a professional indexer or agree to pay the publisher to perform the task.

From this point on, your book and your fate are in the hands of the publisher, and the waiting game continues.

Theoretically, one of the advantages of getting your book published by a royalty publisher (rather than self-publishing) is that the promotion and distribution will be handled by the experts in the publisher's marketing, publicity, advertising, and sales departments. But too often, especially with an unknown author, the publisher's efforts leave much to be desired. Advertising budgets are often minimal, publicity is confined to a few newspaper reviews, and the sales force prefers to concentrate its efforts on books written by the big-name authors.

It's important to be aware of publishing alternatives. This section of *Ten Keys to Writing Success* has been confined to royalty publishers. In most circumstances, royalty publishing offers many advantages to the author: he doesn't have to invest any of his own money, he has professionals who will produce his book, marketing geniuses to promote it, and a sales staff to sell it to the bookstores.

There are, however, various kinds of 'subsidy' publishers which require that the author pay for the publication of his book. Some subsidy publishers serve a legitimate function, issuing technical and special interest books that deserve publication but are so limited in appeal that they cannot be published for a profit. Unfortunately, one segment of the subsidy publishing world attempts to convince the beginning writer that it is legitimate, that it will offer large royalties, and that it will promote and distribute your book, all for a healthy fee, normally $10,000 to $15,000. Companies with this kind of operation are referred to as 'vanity' publishers who make their profits (and they are huge) not from the sale of books to bookstores, but from the unsuspecting author. Claims or promises in vanity literature that the book will be reviewed or promoted stretch the truth to the breaking point. As a rule, reviewers will not look at vanity titles, librarians refuse to take them seriously, and bookstore buyers, upon seeing vanity imprints, will tell you they want nothing to do with them. It's not unusual for sales of a vanity book to be between 25 and 50 copies. And, to coin a phrase, the author (and his book) gets no respect.

It is understandable for an author, after spending years writing a book and then receiving a steady stream of rejections, to grasp at any straw. If he sends his manuscript to a vanity house, he is assured of receiving a letter that tells him in glowing terms what a wonderful book he has written, and for a mere $10,000 their firm would love to publish it.

While publication by a vanity press invites disrepute, self-publishing suffers no such stigma. James Joyce, Thomas Paine, Mark Twain, Walt Whitman and Hart Crane are some of those who ventured into this method at one time or another in their careers. As recent a best seller as Robert Ringer's *Winning Through Intimidation* was self-published initially.

Self-publishing is in no way to be confused with vanity publishing. In self-publishing, the author takes on the entire task himself. Final preparation of the manuscript, copy-editing, design, typesetting, proofreading, manufacturing, registering copyright, publicity, advertising, sales and distribution all must be carried out, either by the author or by someone he hires to perform some of these functions. There are printers who specialize in printing for self-published authors, and some of these will assist in copy-editing, cover and book design, binding and shipping.

Dan Poynter, a successful self-published author, has written the most comprehensive book on self-publishing available today, called, *The Self Publishing Manual.* He lists a number of reasons why an author should consider this alternative: 1) To make more money. If you publish yourself, you receive all of the profit, not the six to ten percent paid by the royalty publisher. 2) Speed. You may be able to self-publish your book in a matter of a few months, compared with the 18 to 24 months usually required by a royalty publisher. 3) Control of your book. You decide on the design, and you are the one to make changes. 4) Self-publishing offers tax advantages. 5) You will gain self-confidence, as the author of a published book.

But unless you have the time, determination and talent to take on all of the aspects of book publishing: production, proofreading, marketing, promotion and distribution, self-publishing may turn out to be a disappointing venture for you.

The royalty publisher solves many of these problems, but the author will help his cause if he is willing to take some action on his own, coordinating with the publisher's marketing division. At the local level, it can pay dividends to contact the book review editors of area newspapers, visit the bookstores and offer to stage an autograph party at their places of business. Obtain the name or names of the publisher's sales representatives in your region and meet with them, providing them with a sales package pointing out all of the pluses of your book. Spend some time with the local librarians who are involved with the acquisition of books for their facilities. Arrange to speak before groups that might be prospective buyers of your book. If there are radio talk shows or cable television programs about books in your area, let the producers know you are available.

Keep in close touch with your publisher's marketing people. The old adage, "The squeaking wheel gets the grease," is surely applicable in this arena. If you have suggestions as to associations, corporate firms, or others with a special interest in your book, let the marketing experts know about them.

Even though your book is being published by a royalty house, you might refer to *The Self Publishing Manual*, in particular those sections devoted to promoting your own book. Some excellent suggestions are also offered in *How to Get Happily Published*, by Judith Applebaum and Nancy Evans.

With all of the hardships, disappointments and disillusionment that may occur when your book is finally published and you realize that the instant recognition you expected doesn't happen, you have taken a major step up the literary ladder. By completing your task, by having your manuscript accepted and published, you have joined a very select group referred to as 'a published author'.

You read the reviews, exulting when they are filled with praise, and dismissing from your consciousness those that are unfairly critical. Even those reviewers who found fault were at least sufficiently impressed to write about it.

Your book, perhaps this one or the next (having proved that you are up to the challenge, there will be a next one), is discovered by the general reading public, and the sales increase, along with the royalty checks. One more step up the ladder, and you are now not only a published author, but a celebrity as well.

Suddenly you find yourself surrounded by new friends, most of whom are eager to have you read their manuscripts or join them at cocktail parties as the guest of honor. Invitations to participate in workshops, appear on talk shows, lecture to local writing groups, and be the main attraction at autograph sessions will be overwhelming. As Jean Rosenbaum writes in *Writer's Survival Guide*, "I was one of the very few authors with a best-selling novel. . . . I was young and foolish, allowing myself to be caught up in a whirl of parties, autograph sessions, lectures and talk show appearances. It was a dream world—people offering instant friendship because of my rank as a celebrity. I overate and drank too much at too many lunches and cocktail parties. A year flew by and I didn't write a word."

Success is defined in the dictionary as the accomplishment of something attempted. If you have completed your book and it has been published, you can legitimately say that you have achieved your objective. But your goal is not to climb a single mountain or win a single race; it is to find on-going, life-long success. You must avoid the temptation to rest on your laurels. The list of authors who have written a best seller and are never heard from again would fill a volume the size of a Michener novel.

Consider your initial success as the first plateau, the foundation for greater achievements. During the production stages of your book, you should start another project, a more ambitious undertaking. In an article in *The Writer*, Dorothy Sayers stressed that literary success carries an obligation of "realism, humility, and loyalty." Only too often, when the royalties start coming, an author loses his perspective and sense of reality. He assumes that the pot of gold is bottomless and takes on a lifestyle and financial obligations that he cannot maintain. Thomas Wolfe, for example, in spite of his prolific output of best-selling works, was constantly in debt, hounding his publishers for more and larger advances in order to meet his obligations. F. Scott Fitzgerald adopted a way of living, along with his alcoholic excesses, that could hardly have been sustained by a Rockefeller.

To retain one's humility in the face of sudden wealth and recognition is another challenge for the uninitiated. Not only does this ability to remain humble affect the writer's personal life, but his future literary endeavors as well. After reading the rave reviews, listening to the flowery introductions and seeing the lines of people waiting for autographs, the author must resist the temptation to tell himself that "I am the greatest." He may be convinced that he has arrived and that every word he writes henceforth will automatically be praised and accepted by his publisher, only to learn that rejection is still a prerogative in the world of publishing, and that success is as nebulous as a floating cloud in the sky.

Your third obligation is loyalty—loyalty to those who befriended you, to those who contributed to your effort, to your agent if you have one, and to your publisher.

Like long lost relatives who suddenly appear at the reading of your rich uncle's will, people who barely acknowledged your existence will come out of the woodwork, shake your hand heartily, refer to you as "my old buddy," and slap you on the back. "I always knew you'd make it," they say, just before asking you for a favor. They'll put pressure on you to speak at a workshop they are sponsoring, or shove a manuscript in your hand and ask you to write an introduction to the book they are writing. "How about putting in a good word about me to your editor?" they'll ask. Published authors should all take a course in "The Art of Saying No."

A special word of caution: Avoid reading manuscripts you'll be receiving from strangers or your new-found friends, lest you be accused at some later date of stealing their ideas.

You'll also be approached by other publishers (most of which probably rejected your material in the past) with offers of large advances and guarantees of greater promotional efforts on your next book. But if you have a good working relationship with the editor who accepted your first book and took the risk with an unknown quantity, and if you were satisfied with the publisher's handling of your work, don't jump to another publisher who tries to woo you with a little more money up front.

Not only is this unethical, but it's bad business as well. If you get the reputation of being an author who jumps from one publisher to another, you may find yourself without a publisher at all. Vera Brittain reminds the newly-acclaimed author, "When your foot is firmly planted on the first step of the ladder, do not forget that your next steps still depend on scrupulousness, reliability, punctuality, loyalty, and decent behavior. . . . And remember that further success will not be obtained by 'wrangles', but by work."

It is time to move on to another plateau, to take the words of Frank Swinnerton to heart: "However successful . . . no authors ever wholly believe in themselves or their successes . . . **They know . . . that however much they try they can never write a book which will truly satisfy themselves.**"

And now, as Thomas Wolfe would say, "I will go everywhere and see everything. I will meet all the people I can. I will think all the thoughts, feel all the emotions I am able, and I will write, write, write."

FOR ADDITIONAL READING

Adler, Mortimer, and Van Doren, Charles, eds. *Great Treasury of American Thought*. R.R. Bowker Co., New York, NY. 1977.

Alkire, Leland G., Jr., ed. *The Writer's Advisor*. Gale Research Company, Detroit, MI. 1985.

Applebaum, Judith, and Evans, Nancy. *How to Get Happily Published*. Harper and Row, Publishers, New York, NY. First Edition, 1978.

Barzun, Jacques, and Graff, Henry F. *The Modern Researcher*. Harcourt, Brace, Jovanovich, New York, NY. Third Edition, 1977.

Bates, H.E. *The Modern Short Story*. The Writer, Boston, MA. 1976.

Biagi, Shirley. *How to Write and Sell Magazine Articles*. Prentice-Hall, Inc., Englewood Cliffs, NJ. 1981.

Blum, Richard A. *Television Writing From Concept to Contract*. Hastings House, New York. 1980.

Bower, Donald E. *The Professional Writer's Guide*. National Writers Press, Aurora, CO. Second Printing, 1984.

Brande, Dorothea. *Becoming a Writer*. Harcourt, Brace and Company, New York, NY. 1934.

Brittain, Vera. *On Being An Author*. The Macmillan Company, New York, NY. 1947.

Burack, Sylvia K., ed. *The Writer's Handbook*. The Writer, Boston, MA. 1986.

Burack, A.S., ed. *Techniques of Novel Writing*. The Writer, Boston, MA. 1973.

Burnett, Whit, and Burnett, Hallie, eds. *The Modern Short Story in the Making*. Hawthorn Books, Inc., New York, NY. 1964.

Campbell, Walter S. *Professional Writing*. The Macmillan Company, New York, NY. 1947.

Campbell, Walter S. *Writing Magazine Fiction*. Doubleday & Company, Garden City, NY. 1948.

Chadwick, H. Joseph, ed. *The Greeting Card Writer's Handbook*. Writer's Digest, Cincinnati, OH. 1975.

Cousin, Michelle. *Writing a Television Play*. The Writer, Boston. 1975.

Erdman, Loula Grace. *A Time to Write*. Dodd, Mead & Company, New York, NY. 1969.

Fadiman, Clifton, ed. *The World of the Short Story*. Houghton Mifflin, Boston, MA. 1981.

Flesch, Rudolf, and Lass, A.H. *The Way to Write*. Harper & Brothers, New York, NY. 1949.

Graves, Robert, and Hodge, Alan. *The Reader Over Your Shoulder*. Vintage Books, New York, NY. Second Edition, 1979.

Gunther, Max. *Writing and Selling a Nonfiction Book*. The Writer, Boston, MA. 1973.

Gunther, Max. *Writing the Modern Magazine Article*. The Writer, Boston, MA. Third Edition, 1976.

Hopwood Lectures. *The Writer and His Craft*. The University of Michigan Press, Ann Arbor, MI. 1954.

Kane, Henry Kane, ed. *How to Write a Song*. The Macmillan Company, New York, NY. 1962.

Lewis, Maxine. *The Magic Key to Successful Writing*. Prentice-Hall, Inc. Englewood Cliffs, NJ. 1955.

Mau, Ernest E. *The Free-Lance Writer's Survival Manual*. Contemporary Books, Inc., Chicago, IL. 1981.

Meredith, Robert C., and Fitzgerald, John D. *Structuring Your Novel*. Harper & Row, New York, NY. 1972.

Meredith, Scott. *Writing to Sell*. Harper & Brothers, New York, NY. Revised Edition, 1960.

Owen, Jean Z. *Professional Fiction Writing*. The Writer, Boston, MA. 1978.

Poynter, Dan. *The Self-Publishing Manual.* Para Publishing, Santa Barbara, CA. Third Edition, 1985.

Preston, Elizabeth; Monke, Ingrid; Bickford, Elizabeth. *Preparing Your Manuscript.* The Writer, Boston, MA. 1986.

Pritchett, V.S., ed. *The Oxford Book of Short Stories.* Oxford University Press, New York, NY. 1981.

Publisher's Weekly. *The Author Speaks.* R.R. Bowker Co. New York, NY. 1977.

Rosenbaum, Jean, and Rosenbaum, Veryl. *The Writers Survival Guide.* Writer's Digest Books, Cincinnati, OH. 1982.

Strunk, William, Jr., and White, E.B., *The Elements of Style.* Macmillan Publishing Co., Inc., New York, NY. Second Edition, 1972.

Swain, Dwight V. *Tricks & Techniques of the Selling Writer.* Doubleday & Company, Garden City, NY. 1965.

Swain, Dwight V. *Film Scriptwriting: A Practical Manual.* Focal Press, London. 1976.

Todd, Alden. *Finding Facts Fast.* Ten Speed Press, Berkeley, CA. Second Edition, 1979.

Walpole, Jane. *A Writer's Guide.* Prentice-Hall, Englewood Cliffs, NJ. 1980.

White, James P., and White, Janice L. *Clarity: A Text on Writing.* Paul Hanson, Publisher, Los Angeles, CA. 1981.

Widdemer, Margaret. *Do You Want to Write?* Farrar & Rinehart, New York, NY. 1937.

Wood, Clement. *Poets' Handbook.* The World Publishing Company, Cleveland, OH. 1946.

Young, Jordan R. *How To Become a Successful Freelance Writer.* Moonstone Press, Anaheim, CA. 1981.